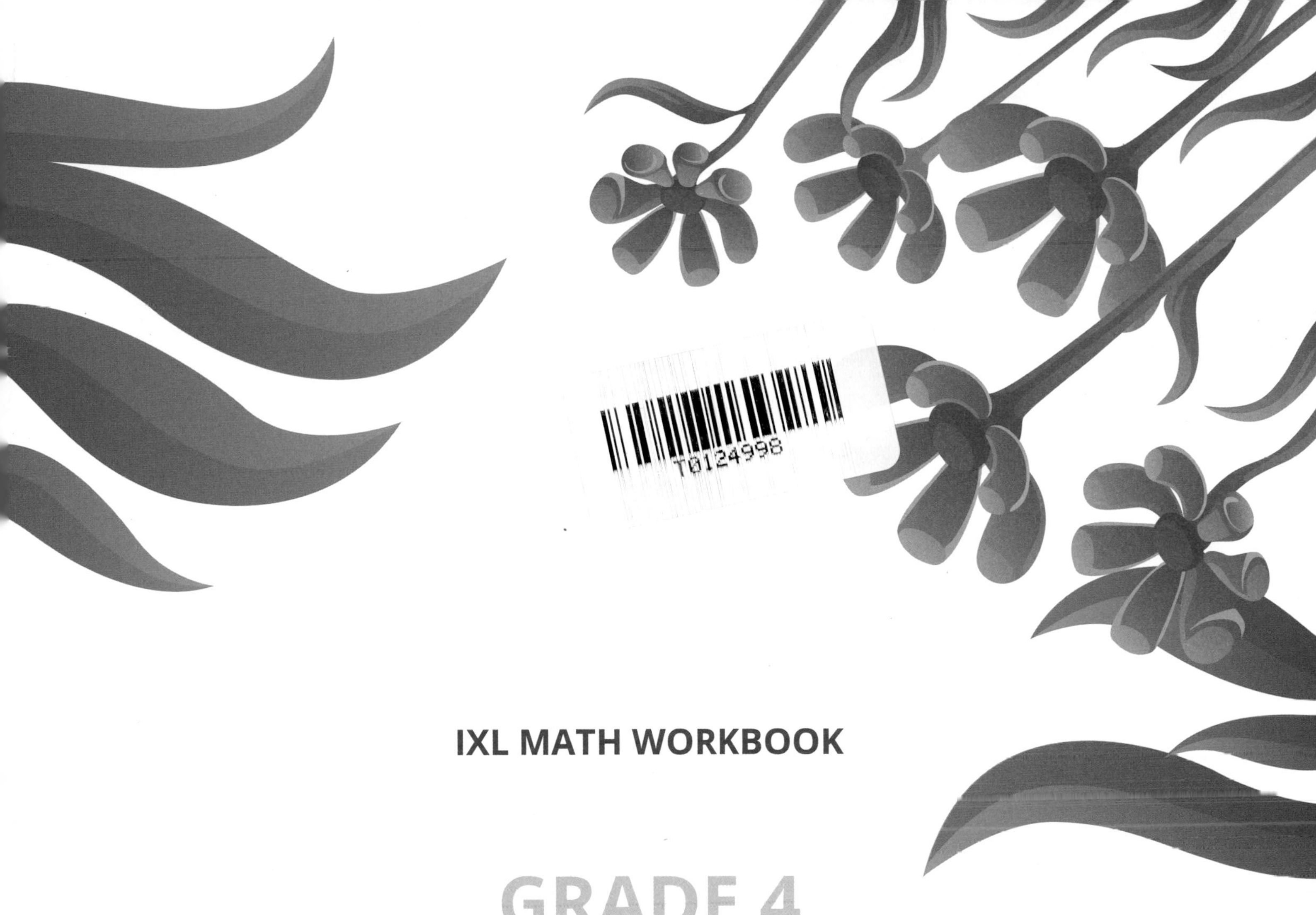

IXL MATH WORKBOOK

GRADE 4

FRACTIONS & DECIMALS

ISBN: 9781947569324
24 23 22 21 20 2 3 4 5 6

Printed in the USA

2 Parts of a whole

Let's Learn!

You can use numbers to represent whole amounts. For example, here is 1 pizza.

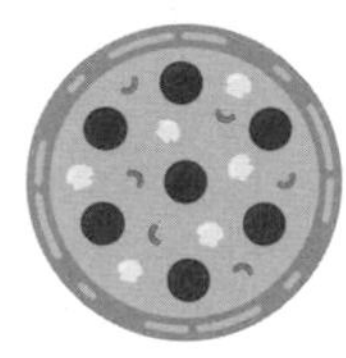

But what if you only have *part* of a pizza? You can use a **fraction** to describe this amount. Here is $\frac{4}{6}$ of a pizza.

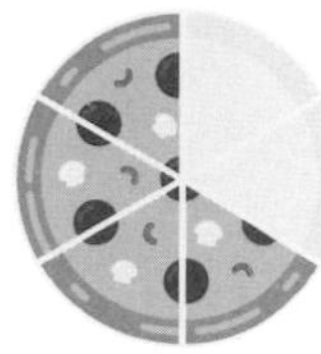

$\frac{4}{6}$

4 ← The **numerator** tells the number of parts you have.

6 ← The **denominator** tells the number of equal parts in the whole.

Write the fraction shown.

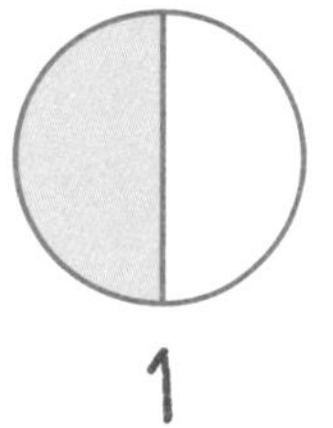

$\frac{1}{2}$

______

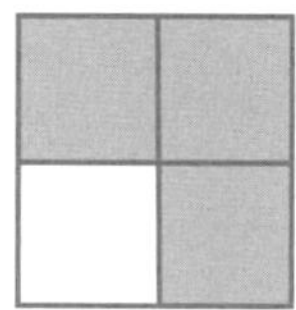

______

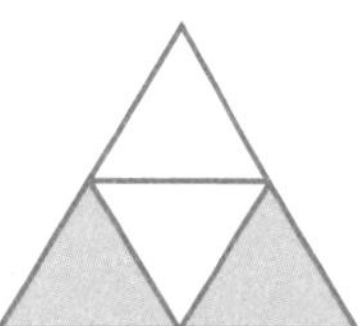

______

______

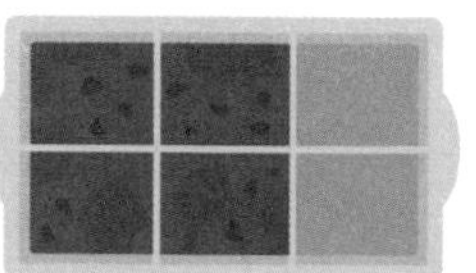

______

IXL.com skill ID **YHL**

For more practice, visit IXL.com or the IXL mobile app and enter this code in the search bar.

Parts of a set

Let's Learn!

You can also use fractions to represent parts of a set. For example, $\frac{3}{6}$ of these animals are dogs.

$\frac{3}{6}$ ← 3 dogs / ← 6 animals

Answer each question.

What fraction of the pencils are broken?

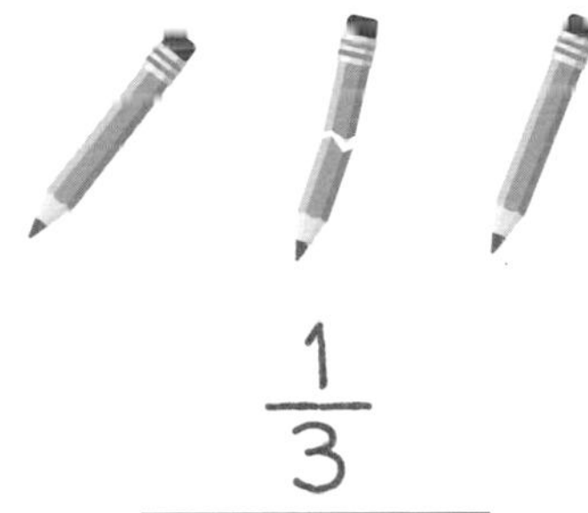

$\frac{1}{3}$ ______

What fraction of the garbage cans are full?

______

What fraction of the balls are basketballs?

______

What fraction of the clothes are shirts?

______

4 Number lines

Let's Learn!

You can show fractions on number lines. This number line shows $\frac{1}{6}$.

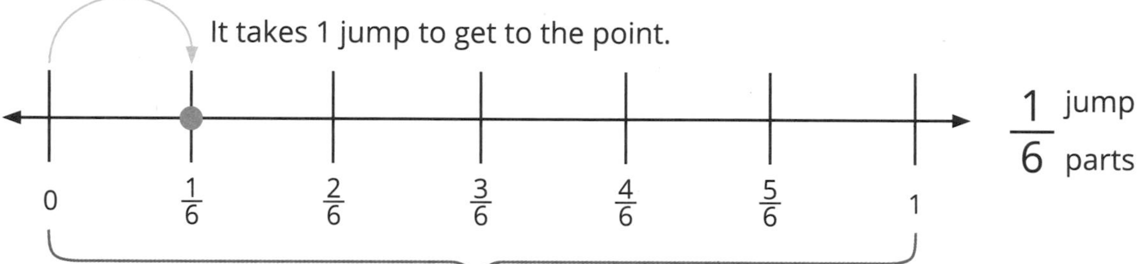

$\frac{1}{6}$ jump / parts

Write the fraction shown.

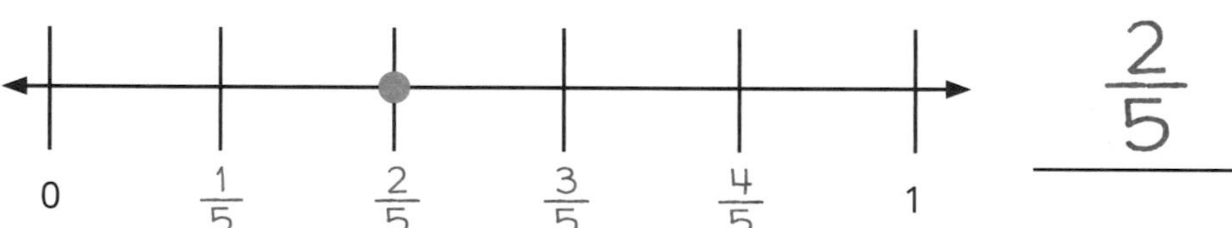

$\frac{2}{5}$

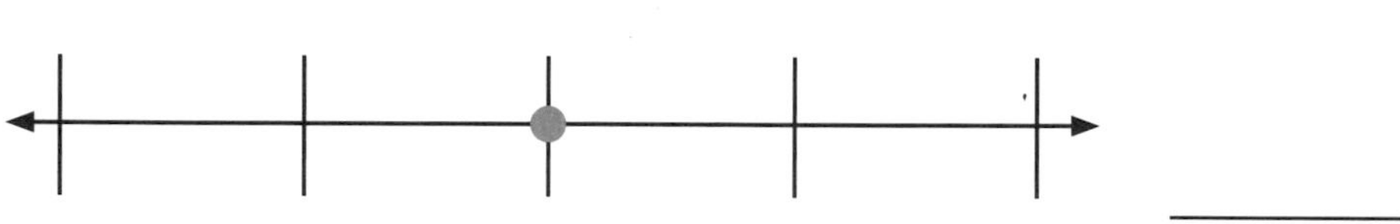

______

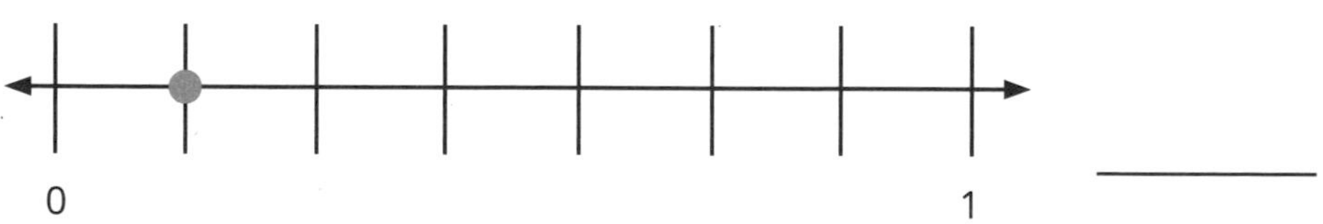

______

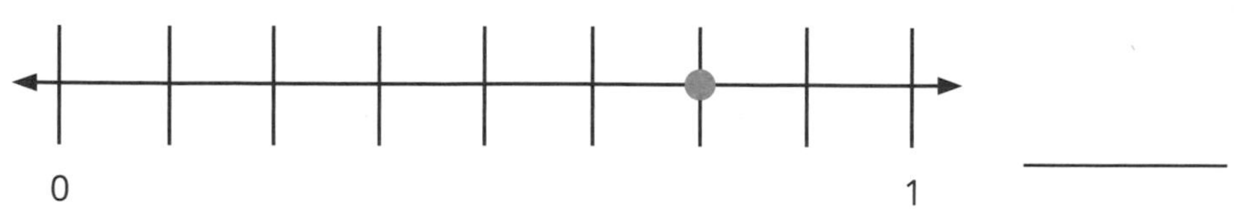

______

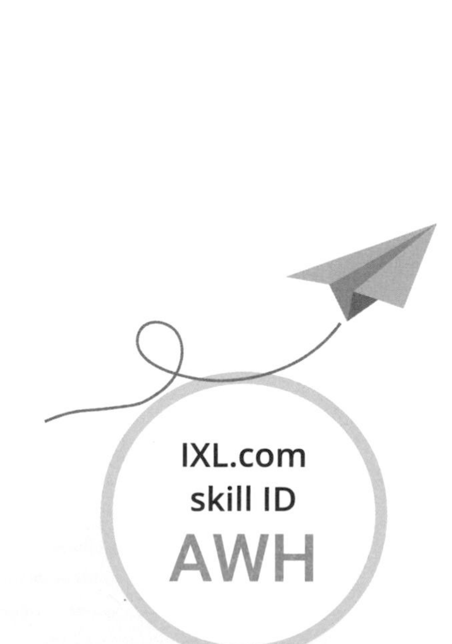

Write a fraction for each model.

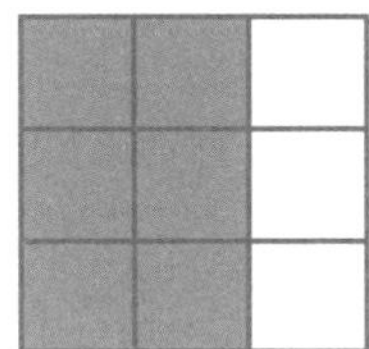

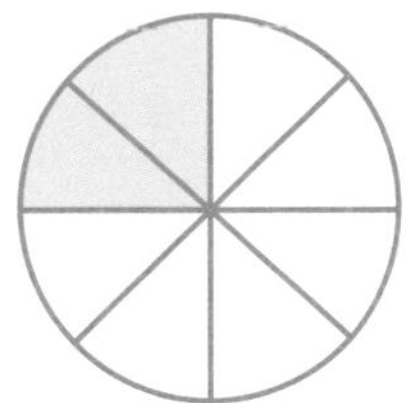

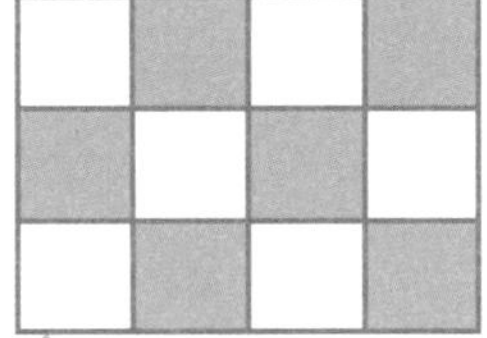

Answer each question.

What fraction of the bottles are ketchup?

What fraction of the shapes are triangles?

What fraction of the foods are fruits?

Write the fraction shown.

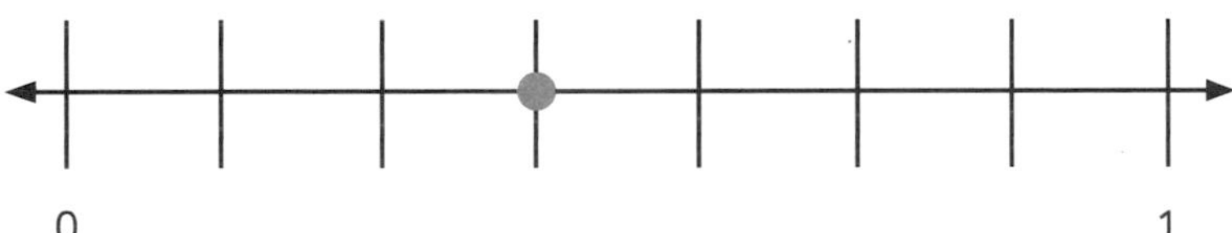

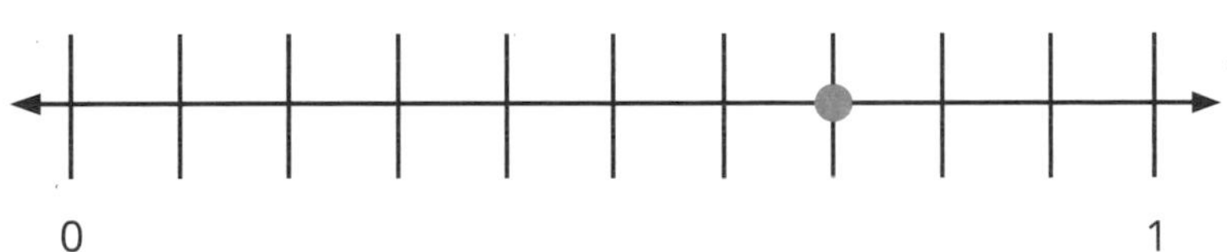

6 Drawing fractions

Shade in each fraction.

$\frac{1}{4}$

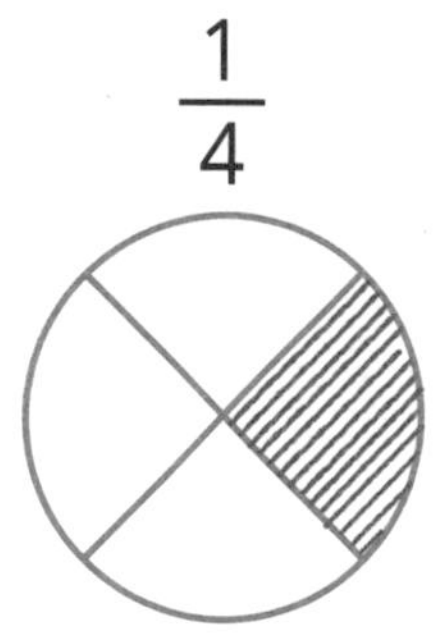

$\frac{3}{10}$

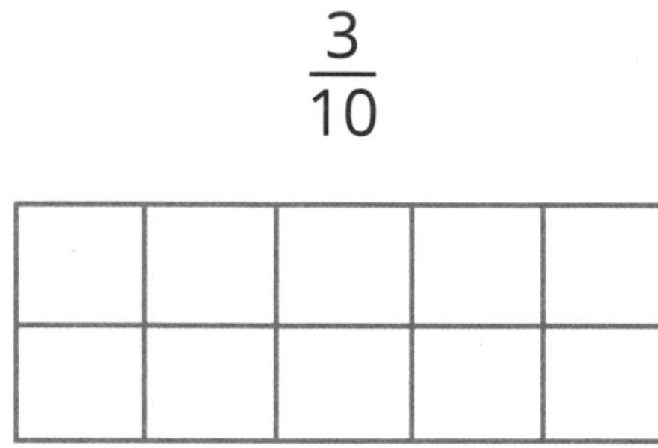

$\frac{4}{5}$

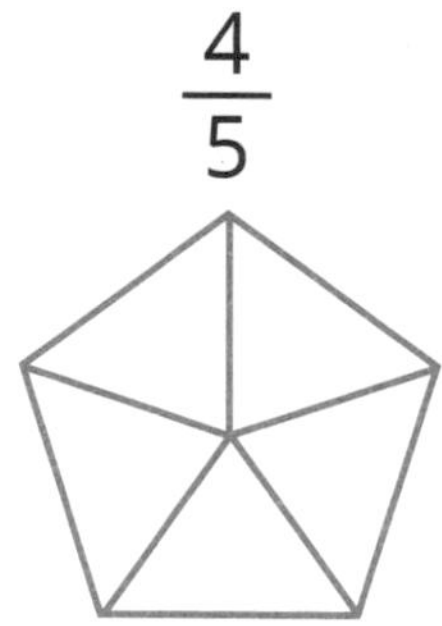

Shade in each fraction.

$\frac{3}{4}$

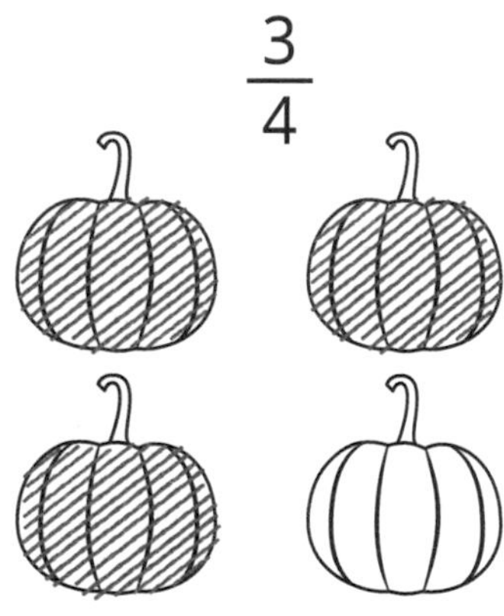

$\frac{2}{3}$

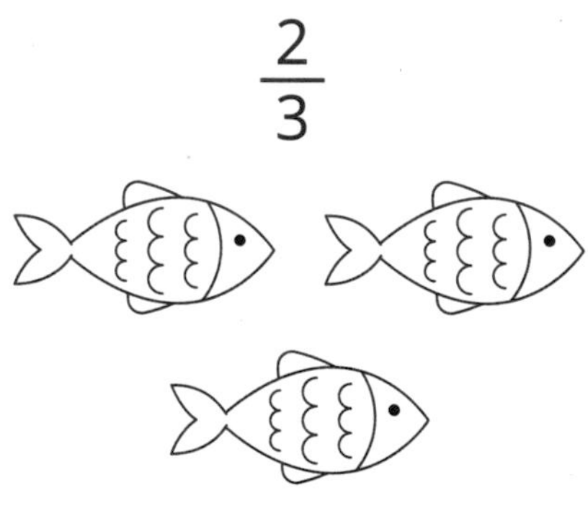

$\frac{4}{8}$

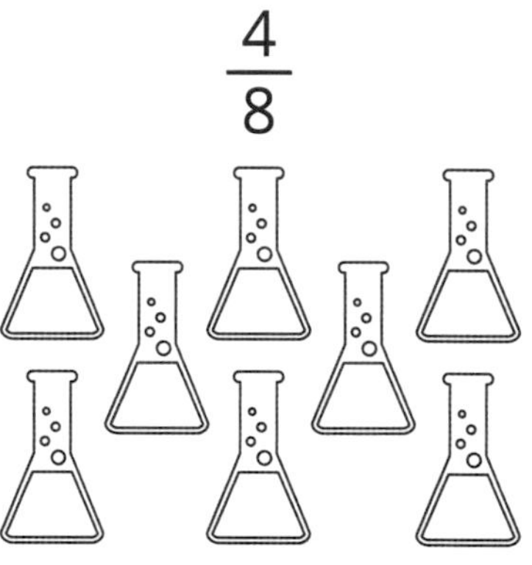

Draw each fraction.

$\frac{4}{6}$

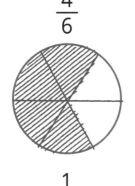

$\frac{1}{3}$

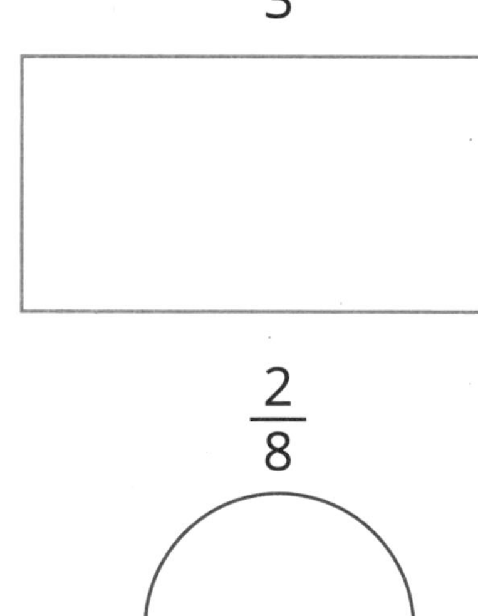

$\frac{3}{4}$

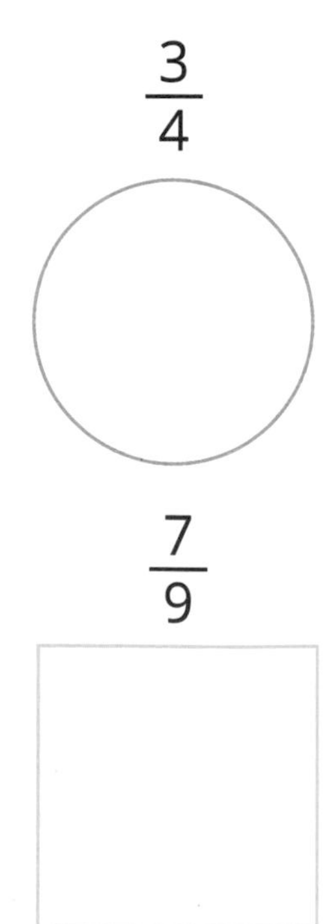

$\frac{1}{4}$

$\frac{2}{8}$

$\frac{7}{9}$

Show each fraction on the number line.

$\frac{1}{6}$

$\frac{2}{8}$

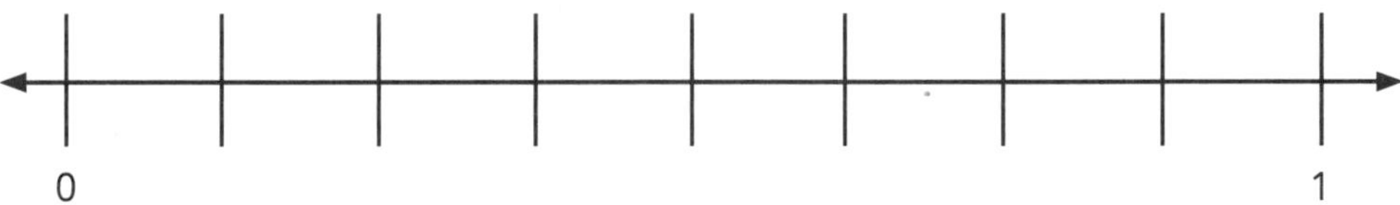

$\frac{4}{9}$

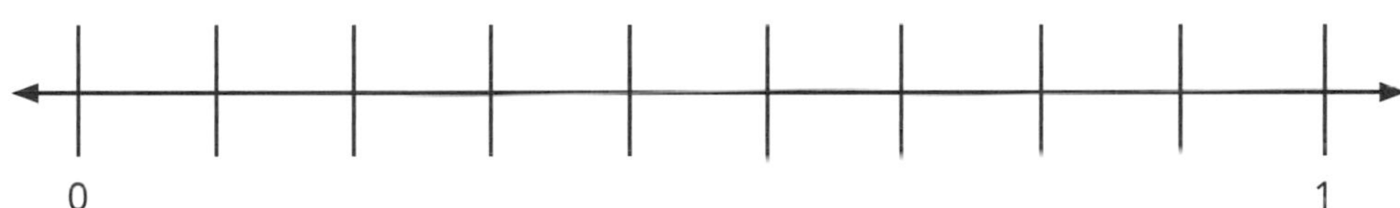

Show each fraction on the number line.

$\frac{3}{5}$

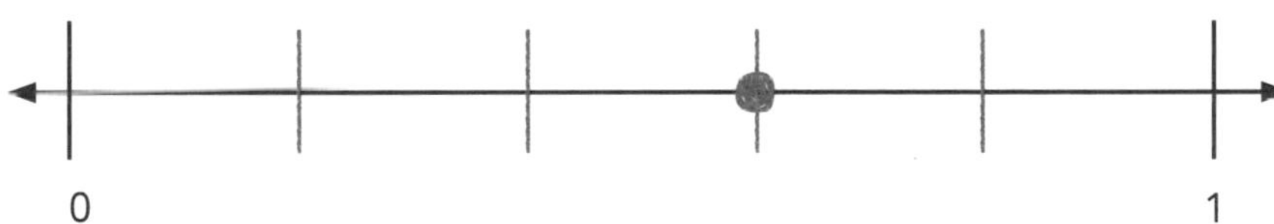

$\frac{1}{4}$

$\frac{2}{3}$

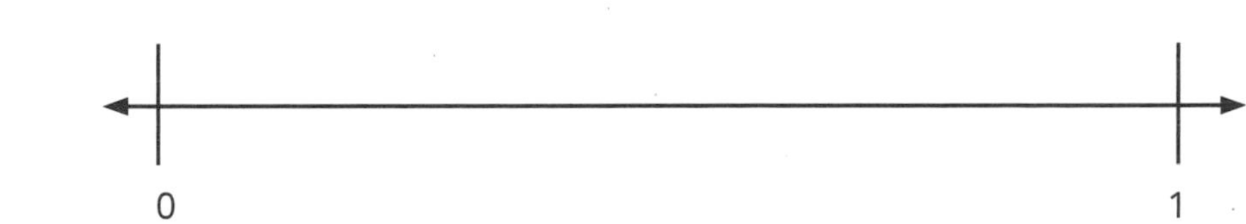

IXL.com
skill ID
7QM

Answer each question.

There are 12 people in a jazz band, and 4 of them play trumpet. What fraction of the band plays trumpet? $\frac{4}{12}$

Maya is listening to an audiobook. She has listened to 7 chapters so far. There are 8 chapters in the book. What fraction of the chapters has Maya listened to already? ______

Noah is painting all 9 of the rooms in his house. He has painted 5 of the rooms so far. What fraction of the rooms does Noah have left to paint? ______

Alex picked 5 cartons of blueberries and 1 carton of strawberries. What fraction of the cartons hold blueberries? ______

In a spelling bee, Charlotte spelled 5 science words and 3 history words. What fraction of the words were science words? 

Let's Learn!

Can you name the parts of the fraction?

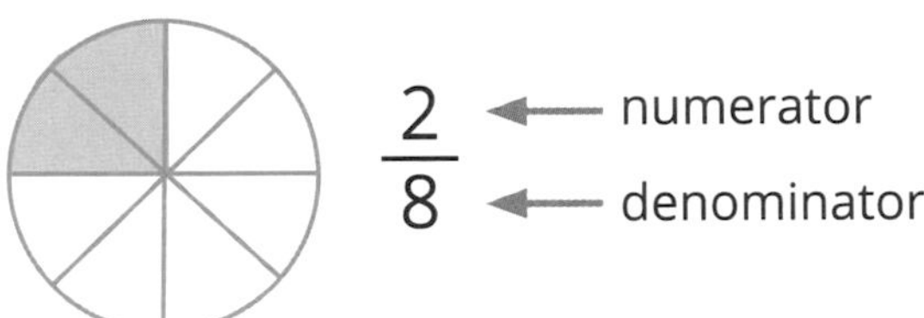

The **numerator** is the number on the top, and the **denominator** is the number on the bottom.

Write a fraction for each problem.

Write a fraction with a numerator of 3 and a denominator of 4. ________

Write a fraction with a denominator twice as large as the numerator. ________

Write a fraction with a numerator of 2 and a denominator of 5. ________

Write a fraction with a denominator that is 1 more than the numerator. ________

Write a fraction with a denominator of 6 and a numerator of 1. ________

Write a fraction with a numerator that is 3 less than the denominator. ________

Equivalent fractions

Let's Learn!

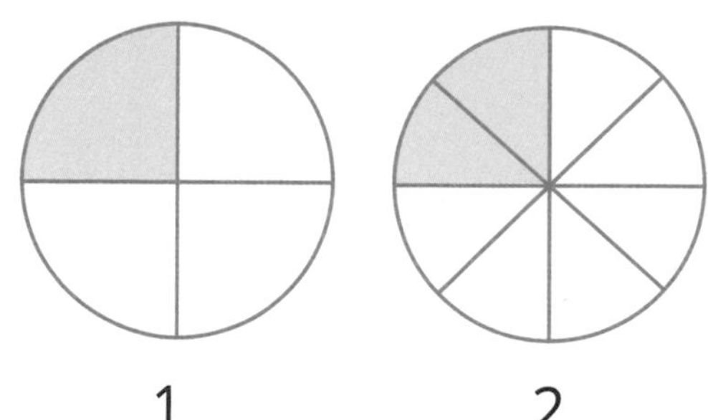

$\frac{1}{4} = \frac{2}{8}$

These pies represent $\frac{1}{4}$ and $\frac{2}{8}$.

These two fractions are **equivalent**, or equal. The same amount of space is shaded in both.

Shade in the equivalent fraction. Write the new fraction.

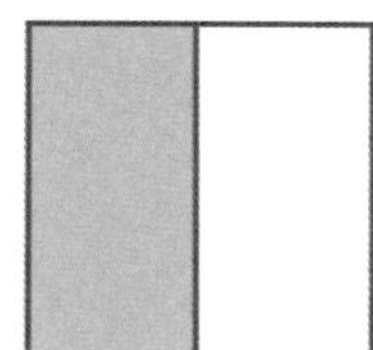
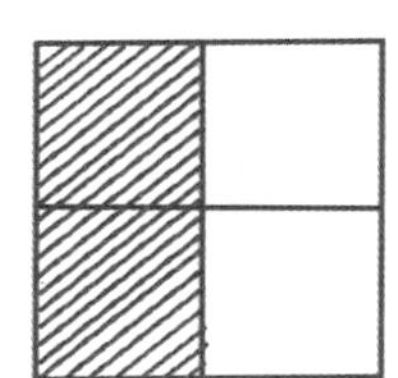

$\frac{1}{2} = \frac{2}{4}$

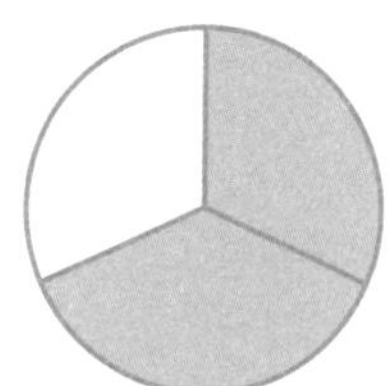
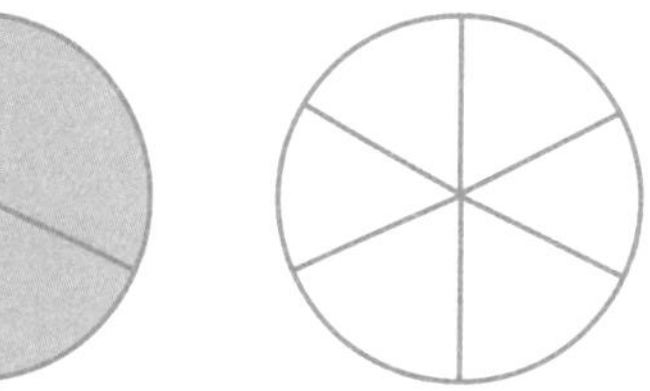

$\frac{2}{3} =$ ______

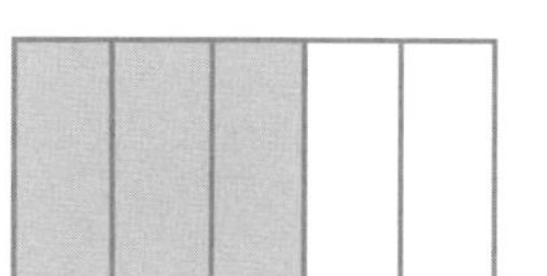

$\frac{3}{5} =$ ______

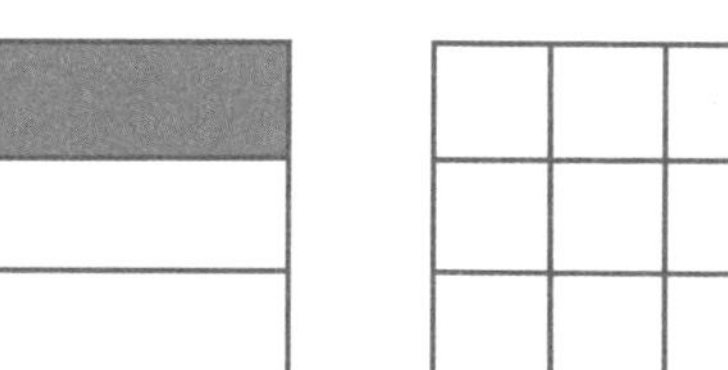

$\frac{1}{3} =$ ______

Shade in the equivalent fraction. Write the new fraction.

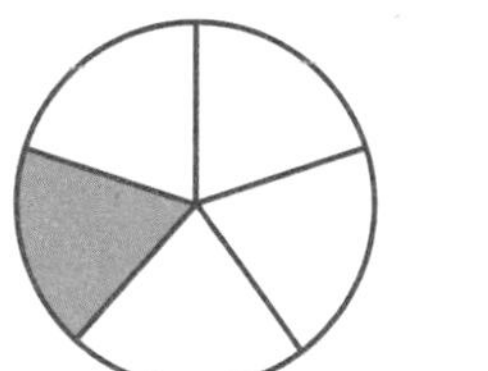 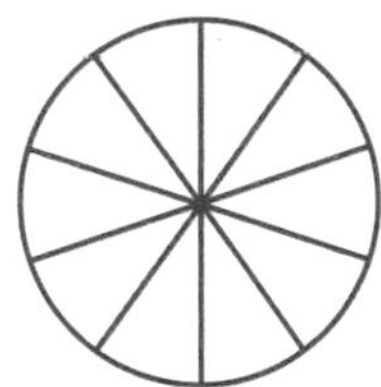

$\frac{1}{5}$ = ______

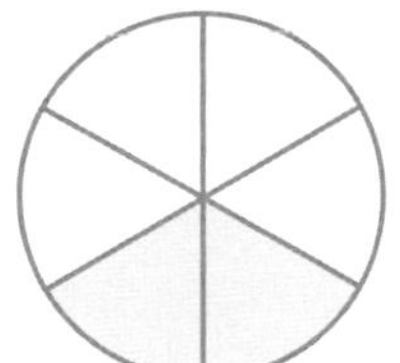 

$\frac{2}{6}$ = ______

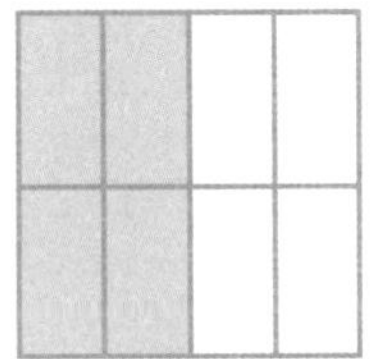 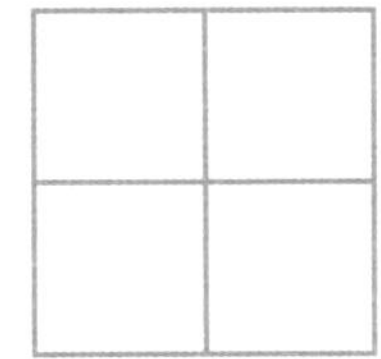

$\frac{4}{8}$ = ______

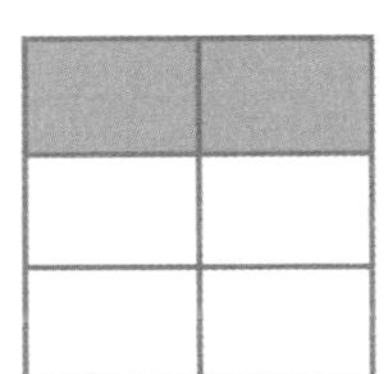 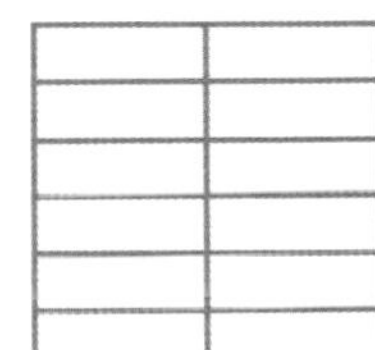

$\frac{2}{6}$ = ______

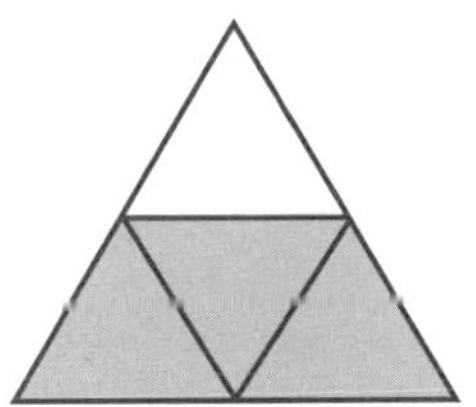 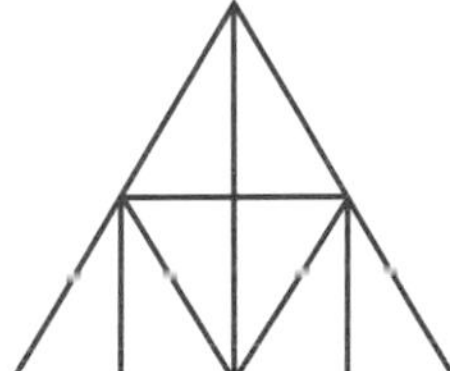

$\frac{3}{4}$ = ______

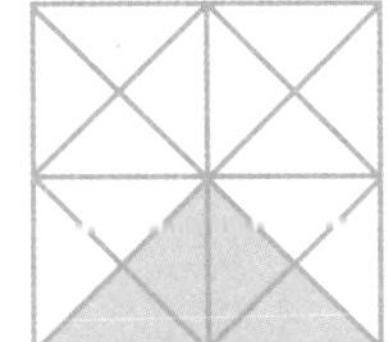 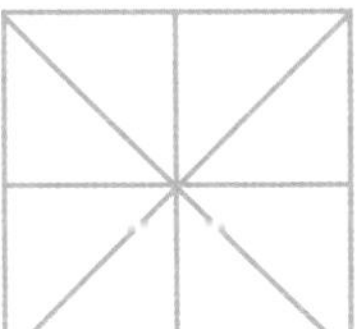

$\frac{4}{16}$ = ______

IXL.com
skill ID
HYC

Equivalent fractions

Show the equivalent fraction on the number line. Write the new fraction.

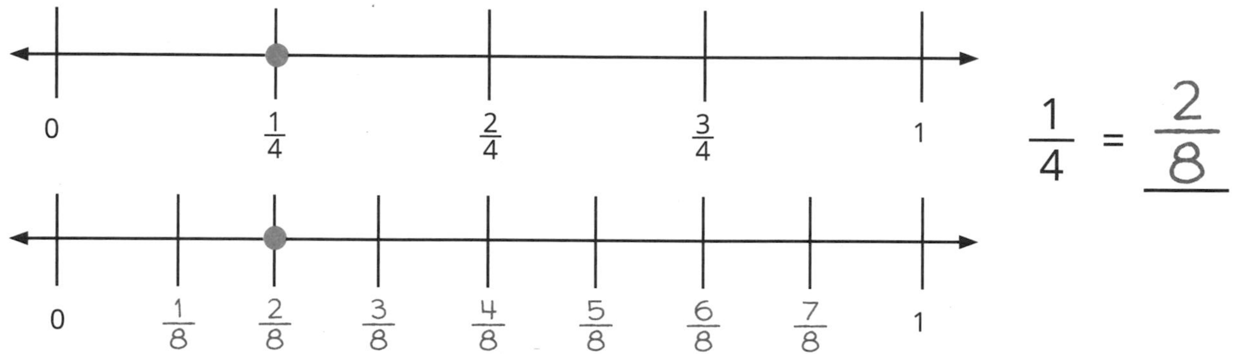

$\frac{1}{4} = \frac{2}{8}$

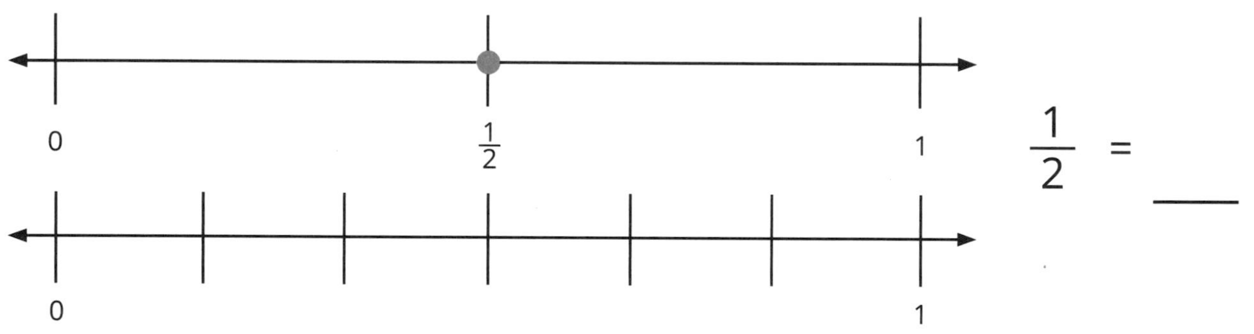

$\frac{1}{2} =$ ____

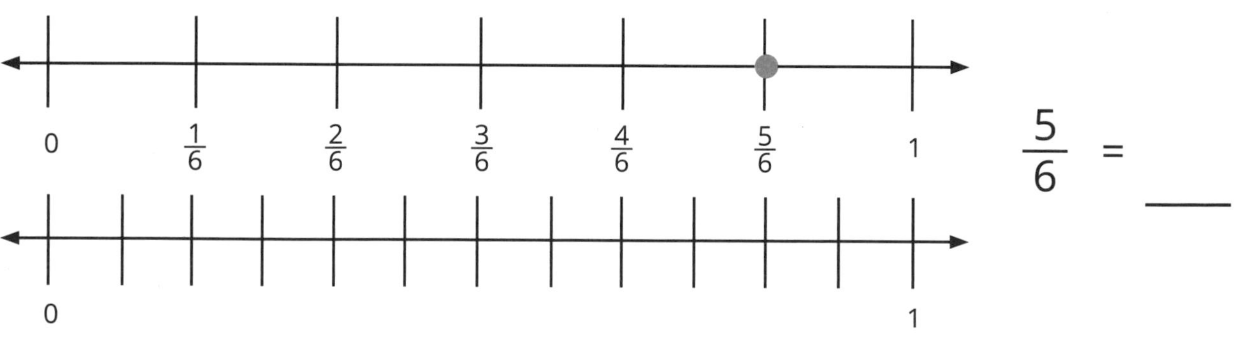

$\frac{5}{6} =$ ____

Equivalent fractions

Let's Learn!

If you multiply the top and bottom of a fraction by the same number, you will get an equivalent fraction.

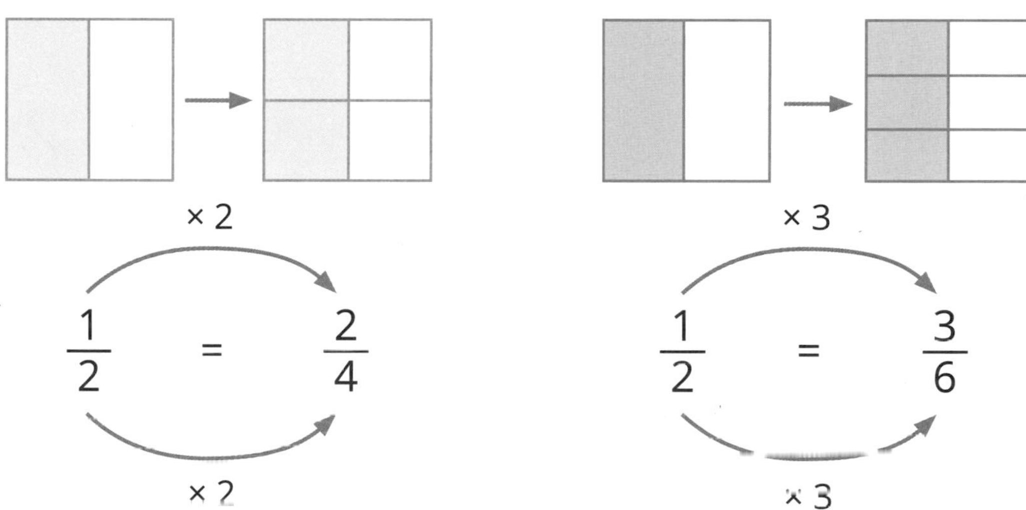

Multiply to make an equivalent fraction.

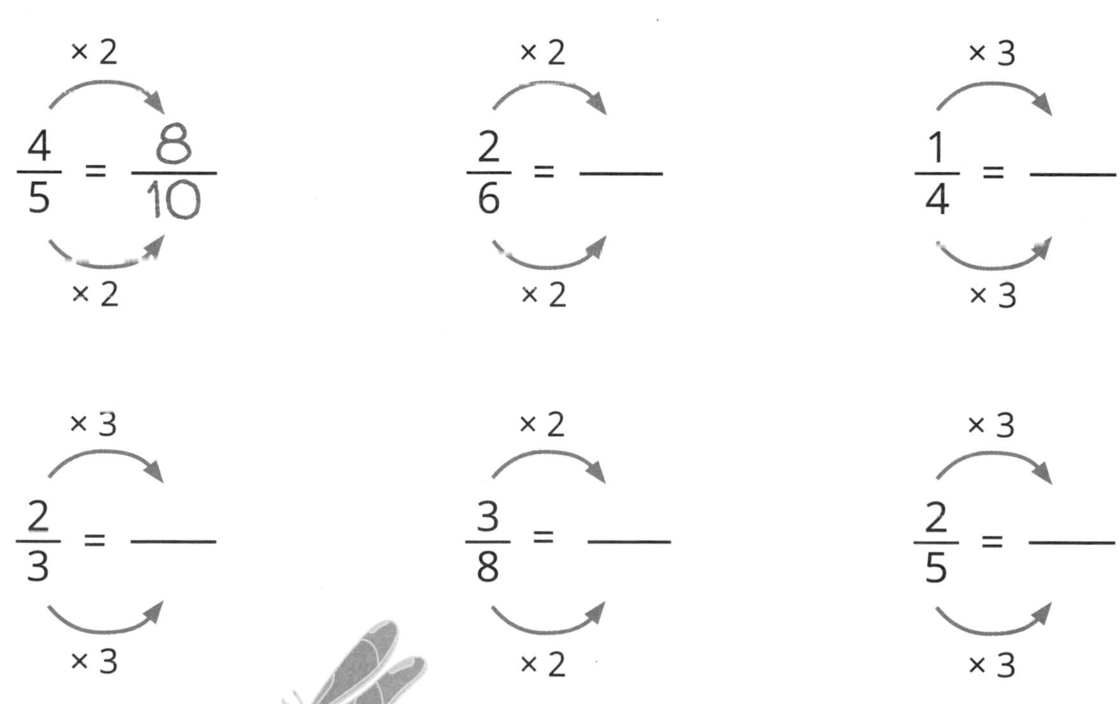

14 Equivalent fractions

Let's Learn!

If you divide the top and bottom of a fraction by the same number, you will get an equivalent fraction. You will need to divide by a number that is a factor of both the numerator and the denominator. Try it for $\frac{3}{6}$.

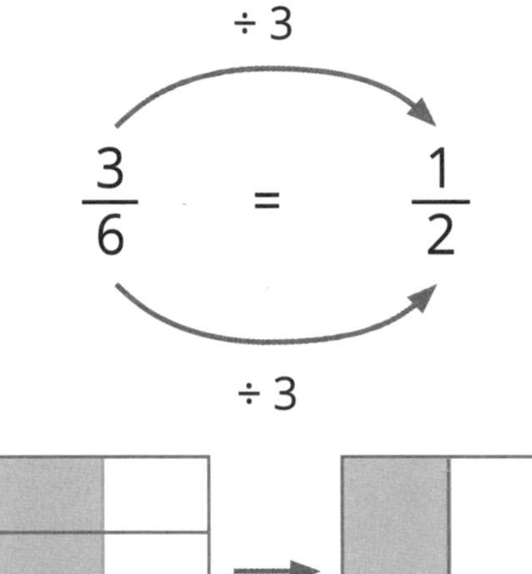

The factors of 3 are 1 and 3.

The factors of 6 are 1, 2, 3, and 6.

So, you can divide by the common factor 3 to get the equivalent fraction $\frac{1}{2}$.

Write the factors of each number. Then divide to find an equivalent fraction.

5: 1, 5

10: 1, 2, 5, 10

$\frac{5}{10} = \frac{1}{2}$ (÷ 5, ÷ 5)

7: ________

21: ________

$\frac{7}{21} = \frac{\quad}{\quad}$ (÷ __, ÷ __)

18: ________

24: ________

$\frac{18}{24} = \frac{\quad}{\quad}$ (÷ __, ÷ __)

Equivalent fractions

Let's Learn!

Remember, multiply or divide the top and bottom of a fraction by the same number to find an equivalent fraction.

$$\frac{5}{6} \overset{\times 3}{=} \frac{15}{18} \qquad \frac{8}{12} \overset{\div 4}{=} \frac{2}{3}$$

(× 3 above and below; ÷ 4 above and below)

Make equivalent fractions.

$\frac{1}{3} = \frac{3}{9}$ (× 3 above and below)

$\frac{5}{6} = \frac{10}{\square}$

$\frac{6}{8} = \frac{\square}{4}$

$\frac{3}{4} = \frac{12}{\square}$

$\frac{12}{18} = \frac{2}{\square}$

$\frac{9}{24} = \frac{\square}{8}$

IXL.com skill ID **7CY**

Equivalent fractions

Write an equivalent fraction for each fraction. There are multiple correct answers.

$\frac{3}{5} = \frac{12}{20}$

$\frac{2}{4} = \_\_\_$

$\frac{2}{3} = \_\_\_$

$\frac{5}{20} = \_\_\_$

$\frac{6}{16} = \_\_\_$

$\frac{4}{18} = \_\_\_$

$\frac{2}{10} = \_\_\_$

$\frac{7}{8} = \_\_\_$

$\frac{12}{16} = \_\_\_$

$\frac{14}{21} = \_\_\_$

KEEP GOING! | Can you write a different equivalent fraction for each problem on the page?

Equivalent fractions

Draw lines to match equivalent fractions.

$\frac{3}{9}$	$\frac{5}{6}$
$\frac{10}{15}$	$\frac{4}{9}$
$\frac{8}{18}$	$\frac{4}{22}$
$\frac{12}{21}$	$\frac{3}{6}$
$\frac{2}{11}$	$\frac{4}{7}$
$\frac{10}{12}$	$\frac{2}{3}$
$\frac{1}{2}$	$\frac{1}{3}$

IXL.com skill ID **GSG**

Simplest form

Let's Learn!

To find the **simplest form** of a fraction, divide the top and bottom by the common factors until you can't anymore.

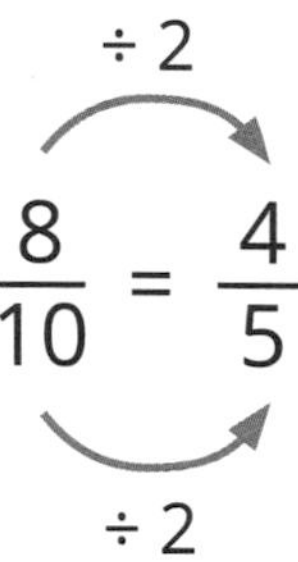

$$\frac{8}{10} \overset{\div 2}{=} \frac{4}{5}$$

For example, the simplest form of $\frac{8}{10}$ is $\frac{4}{5}$.

Tell whether each fraction is in simplest form. If not, write it in simplest form.

$\frac{6}{9}$ NO, $\frac{2}{3}$

$\frac{5}{8}$ ____________

$\frac{3}{4}$ ____________

$\frac{7}{14}$ ____________

$\frac{6}{15}$ ____________

$\frac{11}{16}$ ____________

$\frac{12}{20}$ ____________

$\frac{18}{24}$ ____________

IXL.com skill ID **3R5**

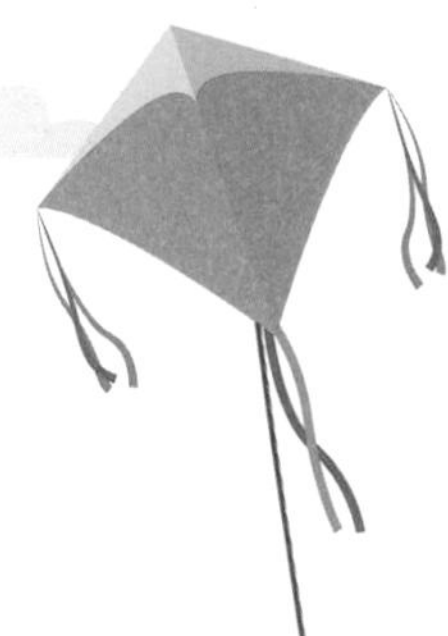

Let's Learn!

When you have two fractions with the same denominator, they have the same number of total parts. You can compare the numerators to see which fraction is bigger. The numerators will tell you which fraction has more of the parts shaded.

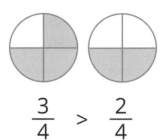

$\frac{3}{4} > \frac{2}{4}$

Compare each pair of fractions. Fill in each circle with >, <, or =.

$\frac{2}{3}$ ◯ $\frac{1}{3}$ (example: >)

$\frac{3}{5}$ ◯ $\frac{4}{5}$

$\frac{1}{6}$ ◯ $\frac{3}{6}$

$\frac{2}{5}$ ◯ $\frac{2}{5}$

$\frac{8}{10}$ ◯ $\frac{7}{10}$

$\frac{5}{9}$ ◯ $\frac{3}{9}$

$\frac{8}{12}$ ◯ $\frac{6}{12}$

$\frac{7}{8}$ ◯ $\frac{5}{8}$

20 Comparing unit fractions

Let's Learn!

A **unit fraction** is a fraction with a numerator of 1. You can compare unit fractions by looking at the denominators. The larger the denominator, the smaller the fraction.

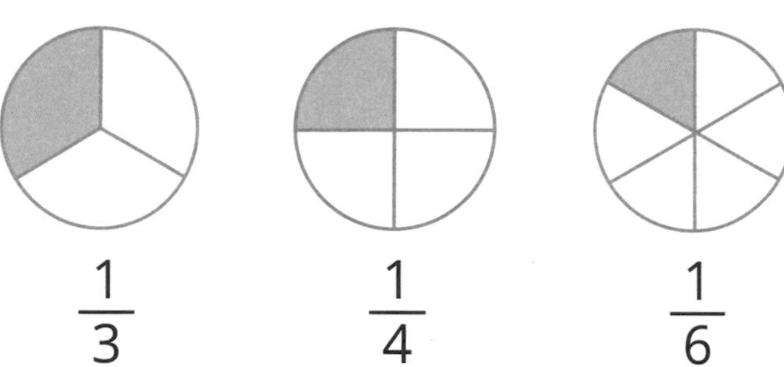

Write each fraction. Fill in each circle with >, <, or =.

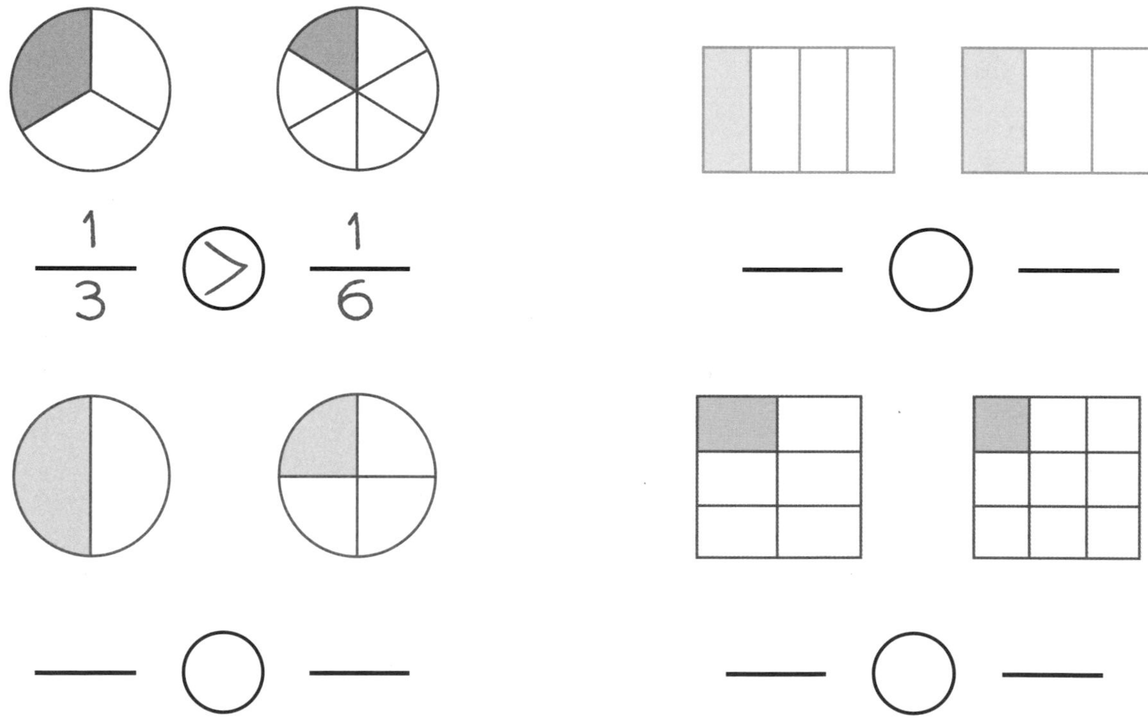

Fill in each circle with >, <, or =.

$\frac{1}{6}$ ◯ $\frac{1}{7}$ $\frac{1}{2}$ ◯ $\frac{1}{3}$ $\frac{1}{8}$ ◯ $\frac{1}{4}$ $\frac{1}{4}$ ◯ $\frac{1}{6}$

Let's Learn!

You can use the rule for comparing unit fractions to compare other fractions, too.

For example, think about $\frac{4}{5}$ and $\frac{4}{10}$. They have the same number of shaded parts, but fifths are bigger than tenths. So, $\frac{4}{5}$ must be greater than $\frac{4}{10}$.

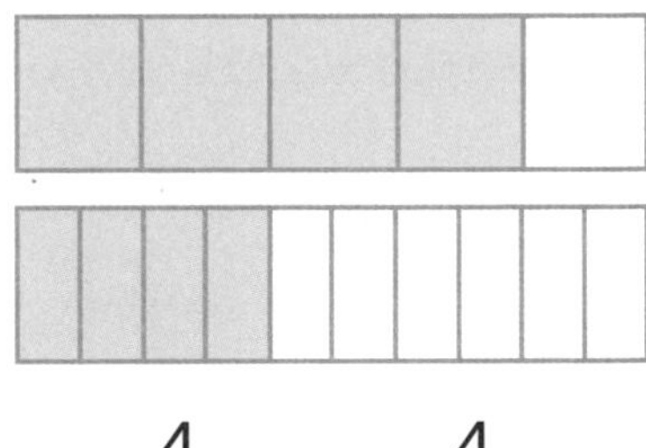

$\frac{4}{5} > \frac{4}{10}$

Fill in each circle with >, <, or =.

$\frac{3}{4}$  $\frac{3}{6}$ $\frac{5}{8}$ ○ $\frac{5}{6}$ $\frac{2}{6}$ ○ $\frac{2}{3}$

$\frac{6}{9}$ ○ $\frac{6}{10}$ $\frac{3}{8}$ ○ $\frac{3}{12}$ $\frac{2}{10}$  $\frac{2}{8}$

Keep going! Fill in each circle with >, <, or =. Think about how big the pieces are and how many are shaded.

$\frac{3}{4}$  $\frac{1}{6}$ $\frac{2}{10}$  $\frac{3}{8}$ $\frac{4}{6}$ 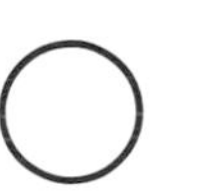 $\frac{3}{7}$

IXL.com
skill ID
M8E

Comparing fractions

Let's Learn!

The fraction $\frac{1}{2}$ is called a **benchmark fraction**. Benchmark fractions are easy to see on a number line. Notice that $\frac{1}{2}$ is easy to see because it is exactly halfway between 0 and 1.

You can compare any fraction to a benchmark. For example, compare $\frac{1}{2}$ and $\frac{5}{8}$. The fraction $\frac{5}{8}$ is farther right on the number line than $\frac{1}{2}$.

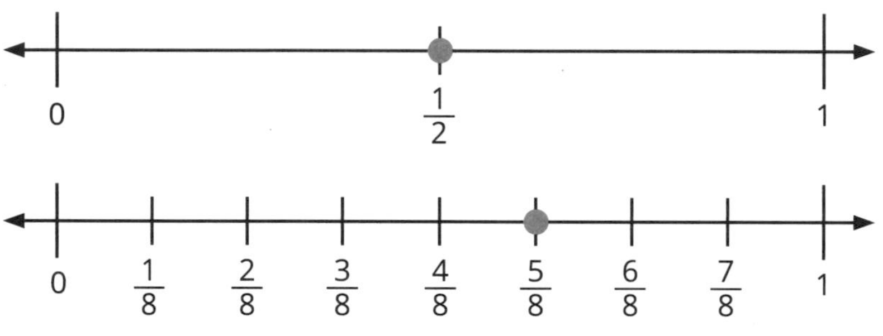

So, $\frac{5}{8} > \frac{1}{2}$.

Fill in each circle with >, <, or =.

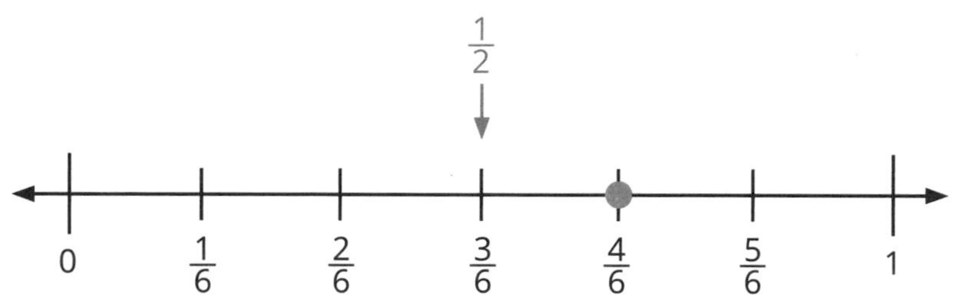

$\frac{4}{6}$ ◯ $\frac{1}{2}$

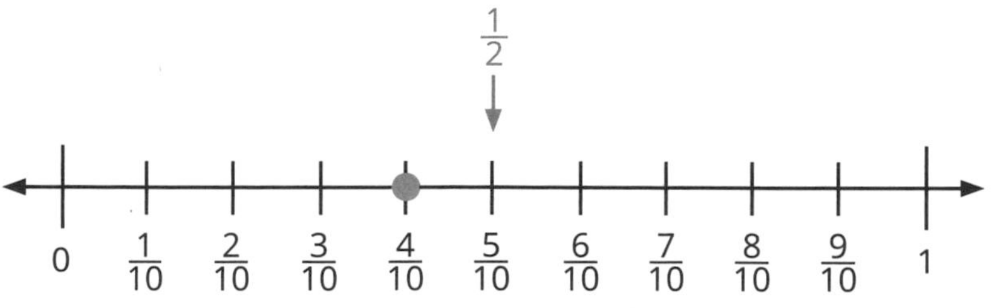

$\frac{4}{10}$ ◯ $\frac{1}{2}$

Circle the fractions that are greater than $\frac{1}{2}$.

$\frac{3}{4}$ $\frac{1}{6}$ $\frac{7}{8}$

$\frac{5}{6}$ $\frac{2}{9}$ $\frac{1}{4}$

$\frac{2}{3}$ $\frac{3}{8}$ $\frac{6}{7}$

$\frac{1}{3}$ $\frac{6}{10}$ $\frac{4}{9}$

$\frac{5}{12}$ $\frac{8}{10}$ $\frac{3}{11}$

Benchmark fractions

Let's Learn!

You can use benchmark fractions such as $\frac{1}{2}$ to compare other fractions. Let's try it for $\frac{3}{4}$ and $\frac{1}{3}$.

First, compare each fraction to $\frac{1}{2}$. You know that $\frac{3}{4} > \frac{1}{2}$ and $\frac{1}{2} > \frac{1}{3}$. So, $\frac{3}{4}$ is greater than $\frac{1}{3}$!

Use $\frac{1}{2}$ as a benchmark to compare each pair of fractions. Fill in each circle with >, <, or =.

$\frac{4}{10}$ ◯ $\frac{5}{8}$ $\frac{7}{8}$ ◯ $\frac{2}{6}$ $\frac{9}{10}$ ◯ $\frac{1}{3}$

$\frac{4}{6}$ ◯ $\frac{3}{8}$ $\frac{2}{4}$ ◯ $\frac{3}{6}$ $\frac{4}{12}$ ◯ $\frac{5}{8}$

$\frac{2}{5}$ ◯ $\frac{6}{7}$ $\frac{4}{5}$ ◯ $\frac{3}{8}$ $\frac{5}{10}$ ◯ $\frac{6}{12}$

$\frac{4}{10}$ ◯ $\frac{5}{6}$ $\frac{6}{10}$ ◯ $\frac{5}{12}$ $\frac{7}{9}$ ◯ $\frac{2}{11}$

IXL.com skill ID **EHJ**

Comparing fractions

Let's Learn!

You can use equivalent fractions to make comparing fractions easier. If you start with fractions with different denominators, try finding equivalent fractions that have the same denominator.

Write equivalent fractions to compare each pair of fractions. Fill in each circle with >, <, or =.

$\frac{4}{8}$ $\frac{2}{4}$ $<$ $\frac{5}{8}$

$\frac{3}{5}$ ◯ $\frac{2}{10}$

$\frac{1}{3}$ ◯ $\frac{2}{6}$

$\frac{6}{12}$ ◯ $\frac{3}{4}$

$\frac{7}{8}$ ◯ $\frac{3}{4}$

$\frac{6}{10}$ ◯ $\frac{1}{2}$

$\frac{5}{12}$ ◯ $\frac{1}{3}$

Least common multiple

Let's Learn!

The least common multiple (LCM) of two numbers is the smallest multiple that the two numbers have in common. Look at these examples.

Multiples of 6: 6, 12, 18, 24, 30, 36...

Multiples of 8: 8, 16, 24, 32, 40...

The LCM of 6 and 8 is 24!

Multiples of 3: 3, 6, 9, 12...

Multiples of 9: 9, 18, 27, 36...

The LCM of 3 and 9 is 9!

You can use the LCM to help compare fractions.

Find the LCM of each pair of numbers. Then use the LCM to make equivalent fractions, and compare. Fill in each circle with >, <, or =.

LCM of 3 and 5: 15

$\frac{5}{15}$ $\frac{1}{3}$ $<$ $\frac{2}{5}$ $\frac{6}{15}$

LCM of 5 and 10: ________

$\frac{2}{5}$ ◯ $\frac{4}{10}$

LCM of 4 and 8: ________

$\frac{3}{4}$ ◯ $\frac{7}{8}$

LCM of 9 and 6: ________

$\frac{5}{9}$ ◯ $\frac{4}{6}$

IXL.com skill ID R7P

Fill in each circle with >, <, or =.

$\frac{2}{5} \bigcirc \frac{3}{10}$ $\frac{1}{2} \bigcirc \frac{2}{6}$ $\frac{1}{3} \bigcirc \frac{2}{6}$

$\frac{5}{8} \bigcirc \frac{3}{4}$ $\frac{5}{6} \bigcirc \frac{7}{12}$ $\frac{2}{9} \bigcirc \frac{1}{3}$

$\frac{7}{12} \bigcirc \frac{2}{3}$ $\frac{5}{8} \bigcirc \frac{2}{4}$ $\frac{7}{10} \bigcirc \frac{1}{2}$

$\frac{6}{9} \bigcirc \frac{2}{3}$ $\frac{1}{2} \bigcirc \frac{1}{3}$ $\frac{2}{5} \bigcirc \frac{1}{2}$

$\frac{3}{4} \bigcirc \frac{2}{3}$ $\frac{3}{4} \bigcirc \frac{4}{6}$ $\frac{4}{6} \bigcirc \frac{5}{8}$

Ordering fractions

Put the fractions in order from least to greatest.

$\frac{1}{2}$ $\frac{5}{6}$ $\frac{2}{3}$ $\frac{1}{2}$ $\frac{2}{3}$ $\frac{5}{6}$

$\frac{1}{6}$ $\frac{1}{2}$ $\frac{6}{7}$ ______ ______ ______

$\frac{3}{4}$ $\frac{3}{8}$ $\frac{1}{2}$ ______ ______ ______

$\frac{1}{3}$ $\frac{7}{9}$ $\frac{4}{6}$ ______ ______ ______

$\frac{2}{3}$ $\frac{5}{12}$ $\frac{3}{4}$ ______ ______ ______

$\frac{2}{4}$ $\frac{2}{5}$ $\frac{1}{3}$ ______ ______ ______

$\frac{2}{6}$ $\frac{1}{4}$ $\frac{2}{3}$ ______ ______ ______

IXL.com skill ID **MSB**

For more practice, visit IXL.com or the IXL mobile app and enter this code in the search bar.

Answer each question.

Stacy and Aaron are reading the same book about the Titanic. Stacy has read $\frac{2}{3}$ of the book. Aaron has read $\frac{3}{4}$ of the book. Who has read more? ______________

Riley has two dogs, Rex and Daisy. Rex has eaten $\frac{5}{8}$ of a cup of food. Daisy has eaten $\frac{1}{2}$ of a cup of food. Which dog has eaten more food? ______________

Penny and Gina are running a race. Penny has completed $\frac{4}{5}$ of the race, and Gina has completed $\frac{7}{10}$ of the race. Who has completed more of the race? ______________

Owen is donating $\frac{3}{12}$ of his old toys to a local preschool, and he is giving $\frac{1}{6}$ of his old toys to his younger brother. Who is getting more of his old toys? ______________

Adding fractions

Let's Learn!

You can add fractions together. Look at the pictures to see how!

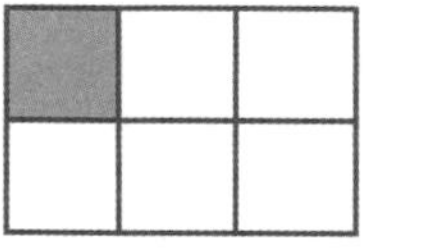
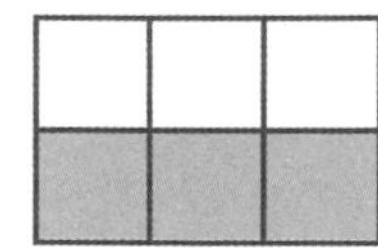
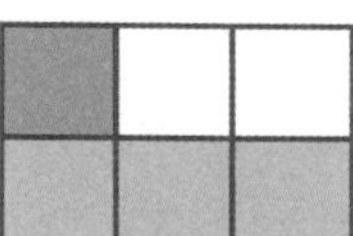

$$\frac{1}{6} + \frac{3}{6} = \frac{4}{6}$$

Add. Shade in the missing fraction.

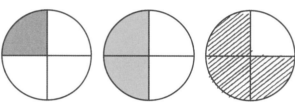

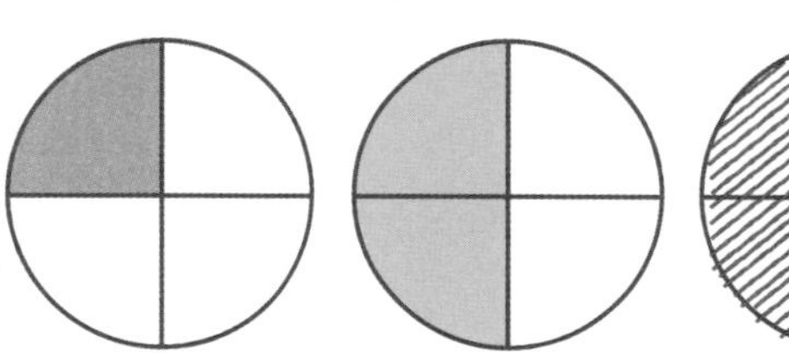

$$\frac{1}{4} + \frac{2}{4} = \frac{3}{4}$$

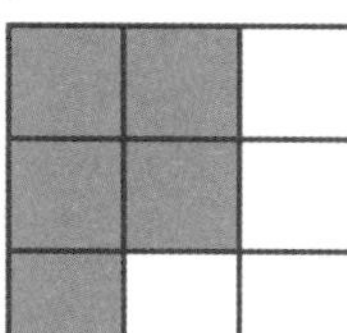
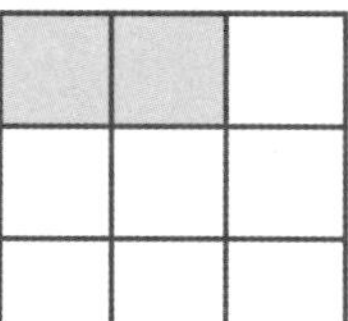

$$\frac{5}{9} + \frac{2}{9} = \text{——}$$

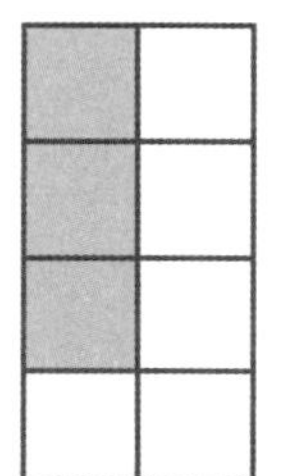
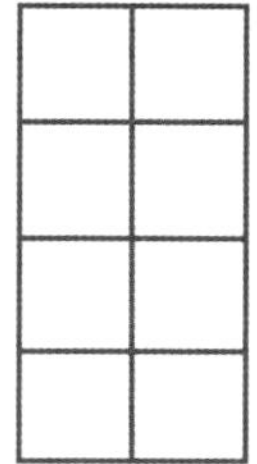

$$\frac{3}{8} + \frac{4}{8} = \text{——}$$

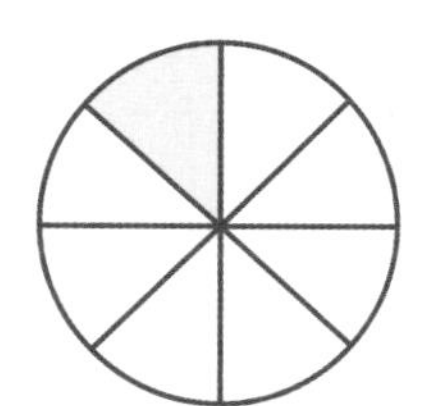

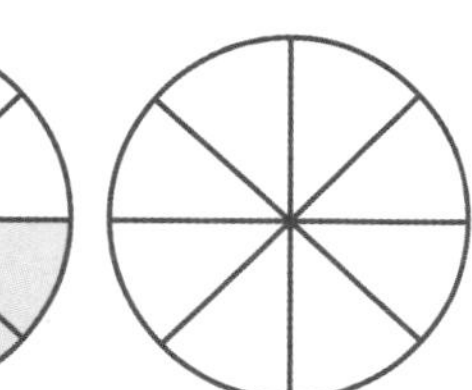

$$\frac{1}{8} + \frac{5}{8} = \text{——}$$

IXL.com skill ID Y5W

TAKE ANOTHER LOOK! Can you come up with a rule for adding these fractions?

Let's Learn!

You can add unit fractions to make other fractions. Remember, a unit fraction is a fraction with a numerator of 1.

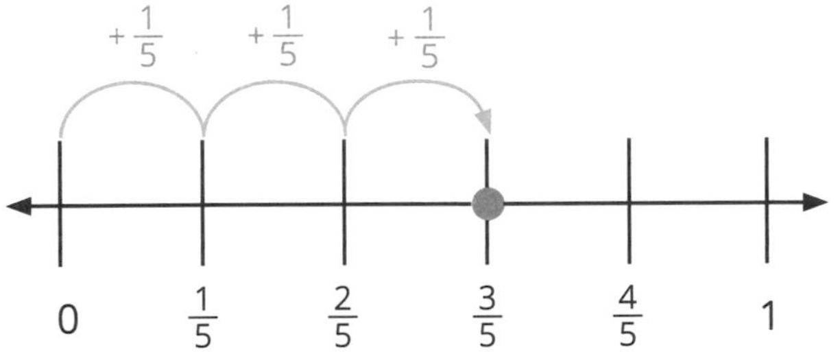

$$\frac{1}{5} + \frac{1}{5} + \frac{1}{5} = \frac{3}{5}$$

Add the unit fractions.

$\frac{1}{4} + \frac{1}{4} = \frac{2}{4}$

$\frac{1}{9} + \frac{1}{9} + \frac{1}{9} =$ ______

$\frac{1}{8} + \frac{1}{8} + \frac{1}{8} + \frac{1}{8} + \frac{1}{8} =$ ______

Write each number as the sum of unit fractions.

$\frac{5}{10} = \frac{1}{10} + \frac{1}{10} + \frac{1}{10} + \frac{1}{10} + \frac{1}{10}$

$\frac{6}{7} =$ ______

IXL.com skill ID XHG

Adding fractions

Use the number line to add.

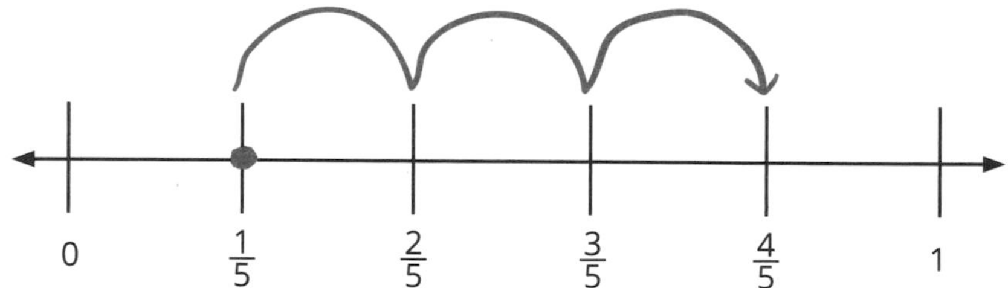

$\frac{1}{5} + \frac{3}{5} =$ 4/5

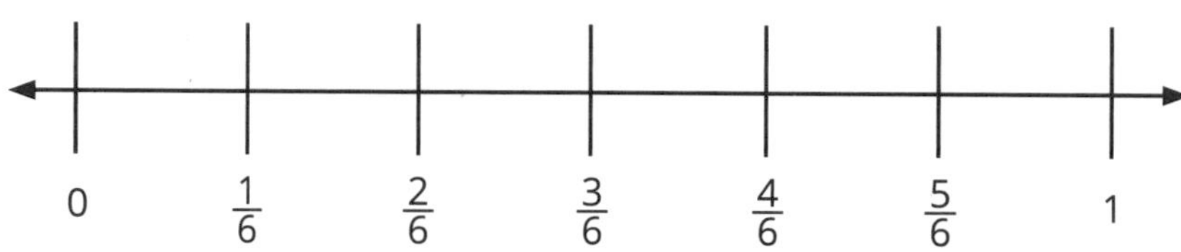

$\frac{2}{6} + \frac{3}{6} =$ ______

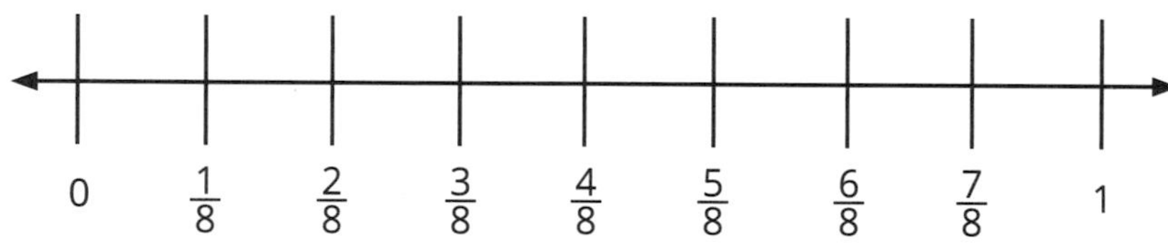

$\frac{2}{8} + \frac{5}{8} =$ ______

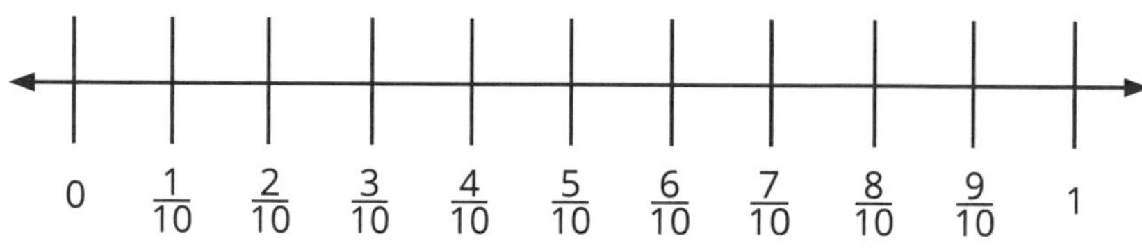

$\frac{4}{10} + \frac{3}{10} =$ ______

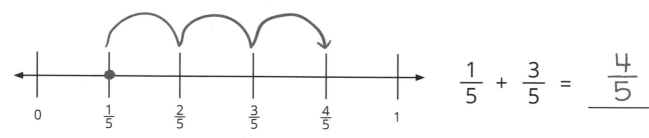

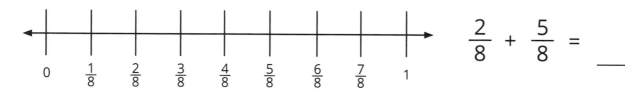

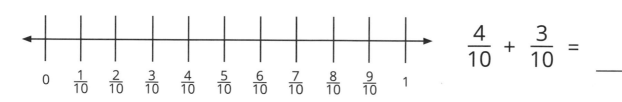

Adding fractions

Let's Learn!

To add fractions with the same denominator, add the numerators. The denominator stays the same.

$$\frac{4}{7} + \frac{1}{7} = \frac{5}{7}$$

Add.

$\frac{1}{8} + \frac{2}{8} = \frac{3}{8}$

$\frac{1}{3} + \frac{1}{3} =$ ______

$\frac{2}{5} + \frac{2}{5} =$ ______

$\frac{3}{6} + \frac{2}{6} =$ ______

$\frac{2}{7} + \frac{1}{7} =$ ______

$\frac{5}{9} + \frac{3}{9} =$ ______

$\frac{1}{5} + \frac{3}{5} =$ ______

$\frac{6}{10} + \frac{2}{10} =$ ______

Add. Fill in the missing numbers.

$\frac{1}{4} + \frac{\boxed{1}}{4} = \frac{2}{4}$

$\frac{\boxed{}}{6} + \frac{4}{6} = \frac{5}{6}$

$\frac{\boxed{}}{8} + \frac{5}{8} = \frac{6}{8}$

$\frac{2}{7} + \frac{\boxed{}}{7} = \frac{4}{7}$

IXL.com
skill ID
PDU

Word problems

Answer each question.

Lia watched $\frac{1}{4}$ of a movie before soccer practice. After practice, she watched another $\frac{2}{4}$ of the movie. What fraction of the movie did Lia watch in all? ________________

Jon's family is on a road trip to the beach. Before lunch, they drive $\frac{5}{9}$ of the trip. After lunch, they drive $\frac{2}{9}$ of the trip before stopping again. What fraction of the trip has Jon's family driven so far? ________________

Ben uses $\frac{4}{12}$ of his garden to plant red peppers. He uses another $\frac{5}{12}$ of his garden to plant yellow peppers. How much of Ben's garden is planted with peppers? ________________

Mrs. Tate ordered a sandwich platter for a class party. Her students ate $\frac{7}{10}$ of the platter. She brought the leftovers to the teacher's lounge, and the teachers ate another $\frac{2}{10}$ of the platter. What fraction of the sandwich platter was eaten? ________________

Add.

$\frac{3}{8} + \frac{1}{8} + \frac{1}{8} =$ $\frac{5}{8}$

$\frac{2}{10} + \frac{3}{10} + \frac{4}{10} =$ ______

$\frac{1}{6} + \frac{2}{6} + \frac{2}{6} =$ ______

$\frac{1}{9} + \frac{3}{9} + \frac{4}{9} =$ ______

$\frac{3}{12} + \frac{3}{12} + \frac{3}{12} =$ ______

$\frac{5}{10} + \frac{1}{10} + \frac{2}{10} =$ ______

$\frac{1}{6} + \frac{2}{6} + \frac{1}{6} =$ ______

$\frac{1}{8} + \frac{2}{8} + \frac{4}{8} =$ ______

$\frac{3}{7} + \frac{1}{7} + \frac{2}{7} =$ ______

$\frac{2}{11} + \frac{4}{11} + \frac{2}{11} =$ ______

IXL.com skill ID LNE

Adding fractions

In the future, you will need to write your answers in simplest form. Try it now! Add. Write each answer in simplest form.

$\frac{1}{6} + \frac{1}{6} = \frac{2}{6} = \frac{1}{3}$

$\frac{1}{5} + \frac{3}{5} =$ ______

$\frac{1}{8} + \frac{3}{8} =$ ______

$\frac{1}{4} + \frac{1}{4} =$ ______

$\frac{1}{3} + \frac{1}{3} =$ ______

$\frac{1}{6} + \frac{1}{6} =$ ______

$\frac{3}{10} + \frac{1}{10} =$ ______

$\frac{4}{7} + \frac{2}{7} =$ ______

$\frac{5}{12} + \frac{1}{12} =$ ______

$\frac{5}{8} + \frac{1}{8} =$ ______

Find the path from point A to point B! You may step only on spaces with sums equal to $\frac{1}{3}$ or $\frac{2}{3}$.

A ↓

$\frac{1}{3} + \frac{1}{3}$	$\frac{1}{8} + \frac{2}{8}$	$\frac{2}{9} + \frac{5}{9}$
$\frac{2}{9} + \frac{4}{9}$	$\frac{2}{3} + \frac{1}{3}$	$\frac{4}{12} + \frac{4}{12}$ → B
$\frac{3}{12} + \frac{5}{12}$	$\frac{1}{6} + \frac{4}{6}$	$\frac{1}{9} + \frac{2}{9}$
$\frac{2}{6} + \frac{2}{6}$	$\frac{1}{6} + \frac{1}{6}$	$\frac{2}{12} + \frac{2}{12}$

Subtracting fractions

Let's Learn!

You can subtract fractions, too! Look at the pictures to see how.

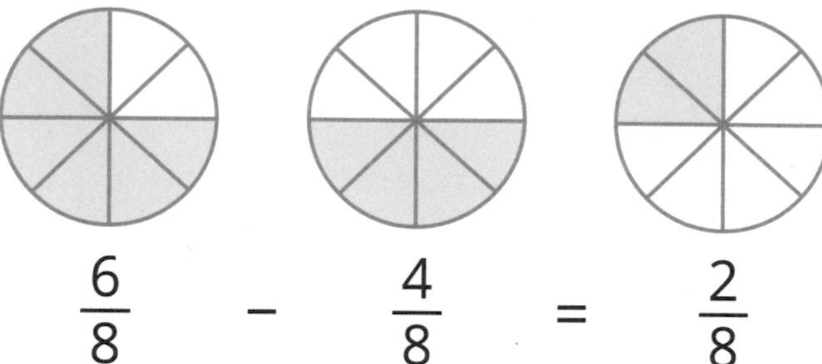

$$\frac{6}{8} - \frac{4}{8} = \frac{2}{8}$$

Subtract. Shade in the missing fraction.

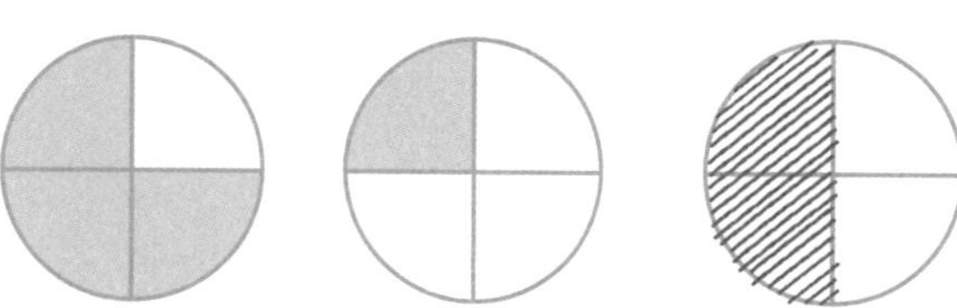

$\frac{3}{4} - \frac{1}{4} =$ 2/4

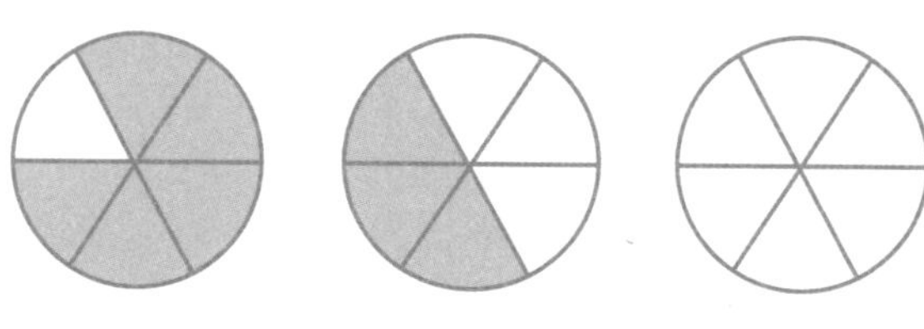

$\frac{5}{6} - \frac{3}{6} =$ ______

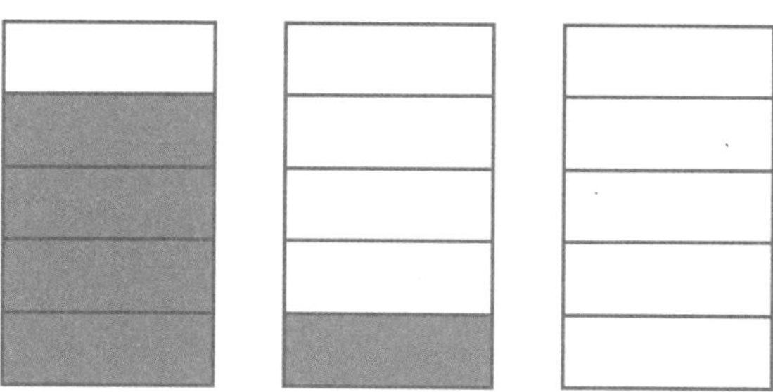

$\frac{4}{5} - \frac{1}{5} =$ ______

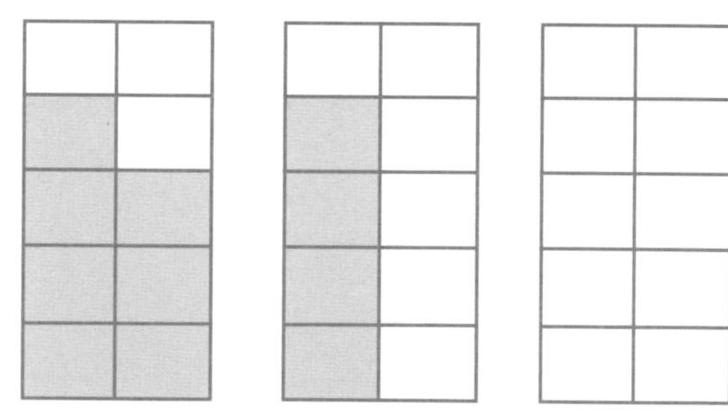

$\frac{7}{10} - \frac{4}{10} =$ ______

IXL.com
skill ID
P99

Use the number line to subtract.

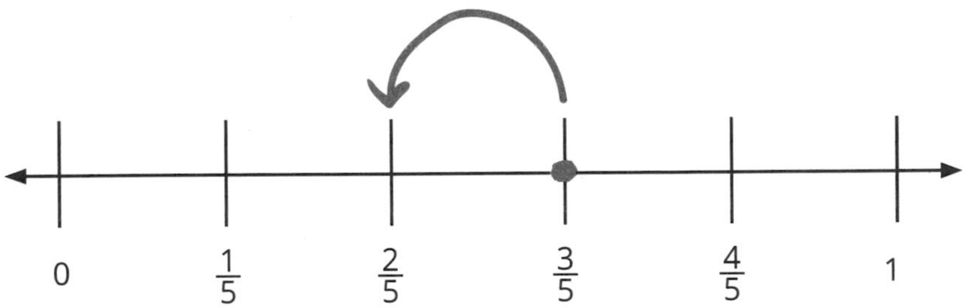

$\frac{3}{5} - \frac{1}{5} =$ $\frac{2}{5}$

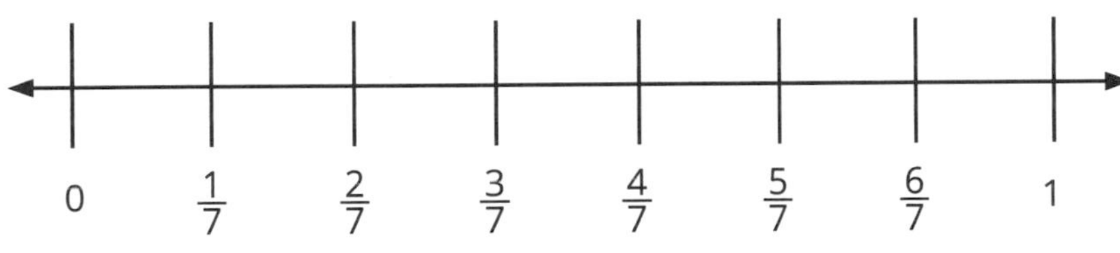

$\frac{5}{7} - \frac{2}{7} =$ ______

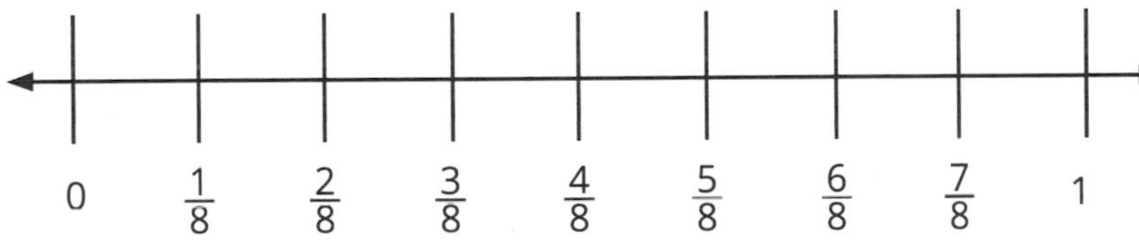

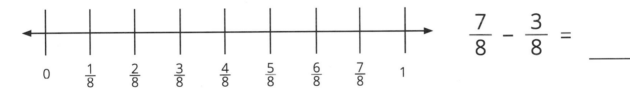

$\frac{7}{8} - \frac{3}{8} =$ ______

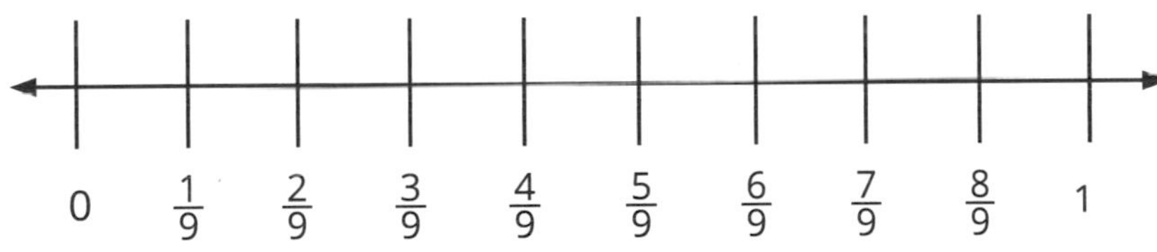

$\frac{8}{9} - \frac{3}{9} =$ ______

IXL.com skill ID **MJX**

Subtracting fractions

Let's Learn!

To subtract fractions with the same denominator, subtract the numerators. Keep the denominator the same.

$$\frac{5}{6} - \frac{2}{6} = \frac{3}{6}$$

Subtract.

$\frac{4}{5} - \frac{1}{5} =$ $\frac{3}{5}$

$\frac{3}{4} - \frac{2}{4} =$ ______

$\frac{2}{3} - \frac{1}{3} =$ ______

$\frac{6}{9} - \frac{2}{9} =$ ______

$\frac{4}{6} - \frac{3}{6} =$ ______

$\frac{8}{9} - \frac{6}{9} =$ ______

$\frac{9}{10} - \frac{3}{10} =$ ______

$\frac{10}{12} - \frac{7}{12} =$ ______

IXL.com skill ID **AVF**

Subtract. Fill in the missing numbers.

$\frac{3}{5} - \frac{\boxed{1}}{5} = \frac{2}{5}$ $\frac{6}{12} - \frac{4}{12} = \frac{\square}{12}$ $\frac{5}{8} - \frac{\square}{8} = \frac{1}{8}$

$\frac{11}{12} - \frac{\square}{12} = \frac{8}{12}$ $\frac{\square}{7} - \frac{1}{7} = \frac{5}{7}$ $\frac{\square}{9} - \frac{5}{9} = \frac{3}{9}$

$\frac{\square}{4} - \frac{1}{4} = \frac{2}{4}$ $\frac{\square}{10} - \frac{6}{10} = \frac{3}{10}$ $\frac{\square}{5} - \frac{2}{5} = \frac{2}{5}$

$\frac{7}{11} - \frac{\square}{11} = \frac{1}{11}$ $\frac{5}{12} - \frac{\square}{12} = \frac{4}{12}$ $\frac{3}{6} - \frac{\square}{6} = \frac{2}{6}$

Challenge yourself! Write numbers to make each sentence true.

$\frac{4}{5} - \frac{\square}{5} = \frac{\square}{5}$ $\frac{\square}{8} - \frac{2}{8} = \frac{\square}{8}$ $\frac{\square}{10} - \frac{\square}{10} = \frac{2}{10}$

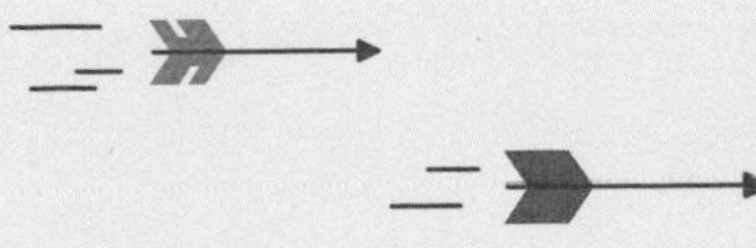

Word problems

Answer each question.

Maggie bought $\frac{11}{12}$ of a yard of fabric. She used $\frac{3}{12}$ of a yard to make a doll dress. How much fabric does Maggie have left? ____________

Liam and his brother are painting the walls of their treehouse. Liam agreed to paint $\frac{5}{8}$ of the walls. This morning, he painted $\frac{3}{8}$ of the walls. What fraction of the walls does he have left to paint? ____________

At Jolie's birthday party, $\frac{6}{8}$ of the cake was eaten. If Jolie ate $\frac{1}{8}$ of the cake herself, how much did the rest of the guests eat? ____________

Noah decided to use $\frac{5}{7}$ of the money in his piggy bank to buy presents for his parents. He used $\frac{3}{7}$ of his money to buy a candle for his mom. What fraction of his money is left to buy a present for his dad? ____________

A brownie recipe calls for $\frac{5}{10}$ of a pound of flour. Logan has $\frac{8}{10}$ of a pound of flour in his pantry. How much flour will Logan have left after he bakes a batch of brownies? ____________

Add or subtract.

$\frac{2}{9} + \frac{6}{9} =$ ______

$\frac{3}{4} - \frac{1}{4} =$ ______

$\frac{4}{5} - \frac{2}{5} =$ ______

$\frac{1}{6} + \frac{3}{6} =$ ______

$\frac{6}{10} - \frac{3}{10} =$ ______

$\frac{7}{12} + \frac{2}{12} =$ ______

$\frac{7}{8} - \frac{4}{8} =$ ______

$\frac{5}{11} + \frac{5}{11} =$ ______

$\frac{3}{10} + \frac{4}{10} =$ ______

$\frac{5}{6} - \frac{3}{6} =$ ______

KEEP IT GOING! | Can you write each answer in simplest form?

IXL.com skill ID **FXD**

Adding and subtracting fractions

Add or subtract. Draw a line between the matching answers.

$\frac{2}{5} + \frac{1}{5} = \frac{3}{5}$	$\frac{7}{8} - \frac{1}{8}$
$\frac{5}{8} + \frac{1}{8}$	$\frac{4}{5} - \frac{1}{5} = \frac{3}{5}$
$\frac{8}{9} - \frac{3}{9}$	$\frac{6}{9} - \frac{4}{9}$
$\frac{4}{5} - \frac{2}{5}$	$\frac{3}{8} + \frac{2}{8}$
$\frac{1}{9} + \frac{1}{9}$	$\frac{1}{10} + \frac{5}{10}$
$\frac{4}{8} + \frac{1}{8}$	$\frac{5}{10} + \frac{3}{10}$
$\frac{9}{10} - \frac{1}{10}$	$\frac{6}{9} - \frac{1}{9}$
$\frac{3}{10} + \frac{3}{10}$	$\frac{1}{5} + \frac{1}{5}$

Mia came up with her own recipe for macarons. Answer each question.

Mia's Macarons

2 cups powdered sugar

$\frac{6}{8}$ cup almond flour

$\frac{2}{8}$ cup granulated sugar

3 egg whites

$\frac{3}{4}$ teaspoon vanilla extract

Chocolate filling

$\frac{4}{12}$ cup heavy cream

$\frac{6}{12}$ cup melted chocolate

Mia had $\frac{7}{8}$ of a cup of almond flour in her pantry. How much almond flour did she have left after making the macarons? __________

Mia poured $\frac{1}{8}$ of a cup of granulated sugar into the bowl. How much more granulated sugar does she need to add? __________

Mia measured out $\frac{1}{4}$ of a teaspoon of vanilla extract. How much more will she need to add? __________

Mia heated up the heavy cream and mixed in the melted chocolate to make the chocolate filling. How much chocolate filling was there? __________

Adding and subtracting fractions

Add or subtract.

$\frac{5}{20} + \frac{7}{20} =$ $\frac{12}{20}$

$\frac{10}{40} - \frac{5}{40} =$ ______

$\frac{8}{54} + \frac{6}{54} =$ ______

$\frac{9}{25} + \frac{7}{25} =$ ______

$\frac{11}{30} + \frac{12}{30} =$ ______

$\frac{17}{19} - \frac{14}{19} =$ ______

$\frac{45}{50} - \frac{32}{50} =$ ______

$\frac{28}{35} - \frac{14}{35} =$ ______

$\frac{56}{90} + \frac{31}{90} =$ ______

$\frac{72}{80} - \frac{59}{80} =$ ______

KEEP IT GOING! | For an extra challenge, write each answer in simplest form!

IXL.com skill ID **FXW**

Adding with unlike denominators

Let's Learn!

To add fractions with different denominators, make equivalent fractions with the same denominator. Then add!

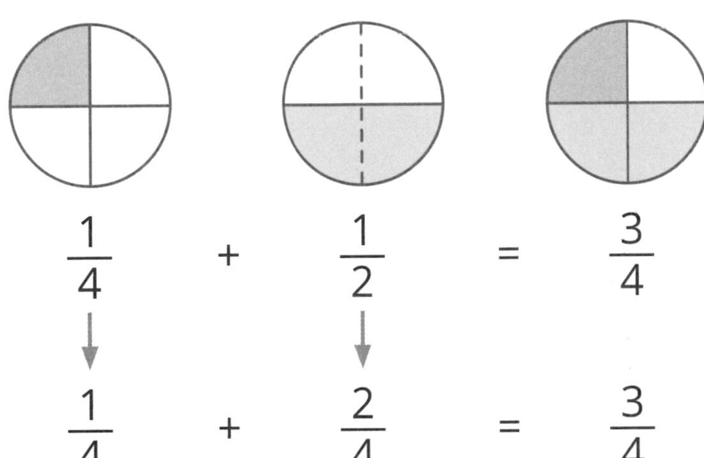

$$\frac{1}{4} + \frac{1}{2} = \frac{3}{4}$$

$$\frac{1}{4} + \frac{2}{4} = \frac{3}{4}$$

Add.

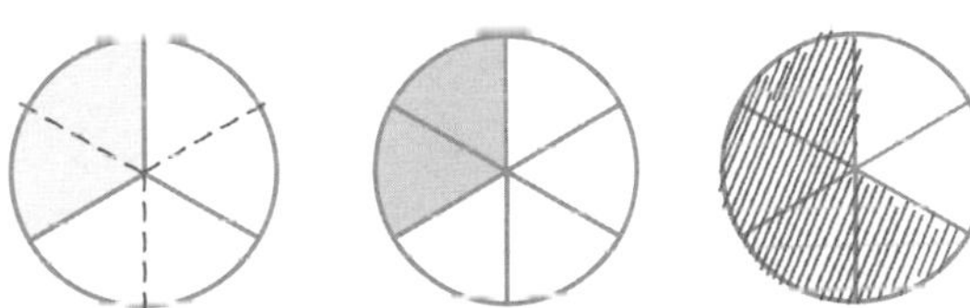

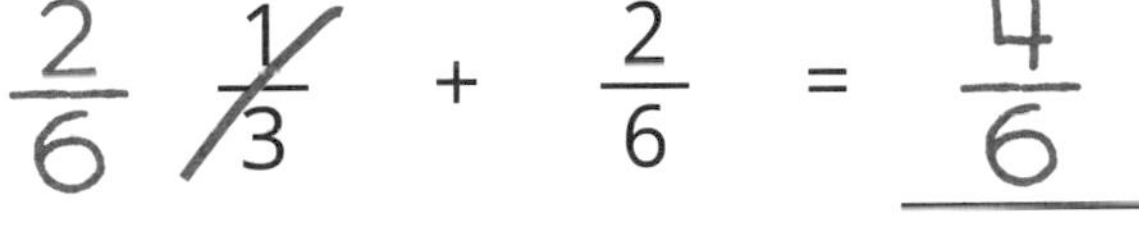

$\frac{1}{3} + \frac{2}{6} =$ ______

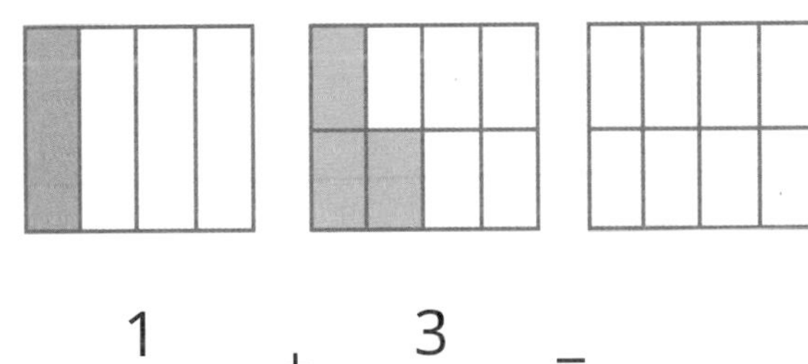

$\frac{1}{4} + \frac{3}{8} =$ ______

$\frac{2}{9} + \frac{2}{3} =$ ______

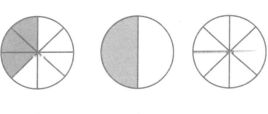

$\frac{3}{8} + \frac{1}{2} =$ ______

IXL.com skill ID **6PM**

Adding with unlike denominators

Add.

$\frac{1}{3} + \frac{1}{4} = \frac{7}{12}$

$\frac{4}{12}$ $\frac{3}{12}$

$\frac{1}{5} + \frac{1}{2} =$ ______

$\frac{1}{7} + \frac{2}{3} =$ ______

$\frac{2}{6} + \frac{2}{4} =$ ______

$\frac{1}{4} + \frac{2}{6} =$ ______

$\frac{2}{3} + \frac{1}{4} =$ ______

$\frac{2}{3} + \frac{1}{5} =$ ______

$\frac{1}{2} + \frac{3}{7} =$ ______

IXL.com skill ID **7BJ**

Let's Learn!

Mixed numbers are numbers that have a whole number part and a fraction part.

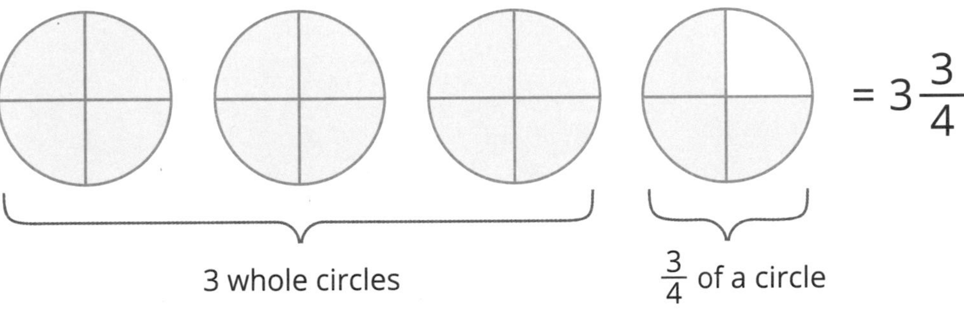

Write the mixed number shown.

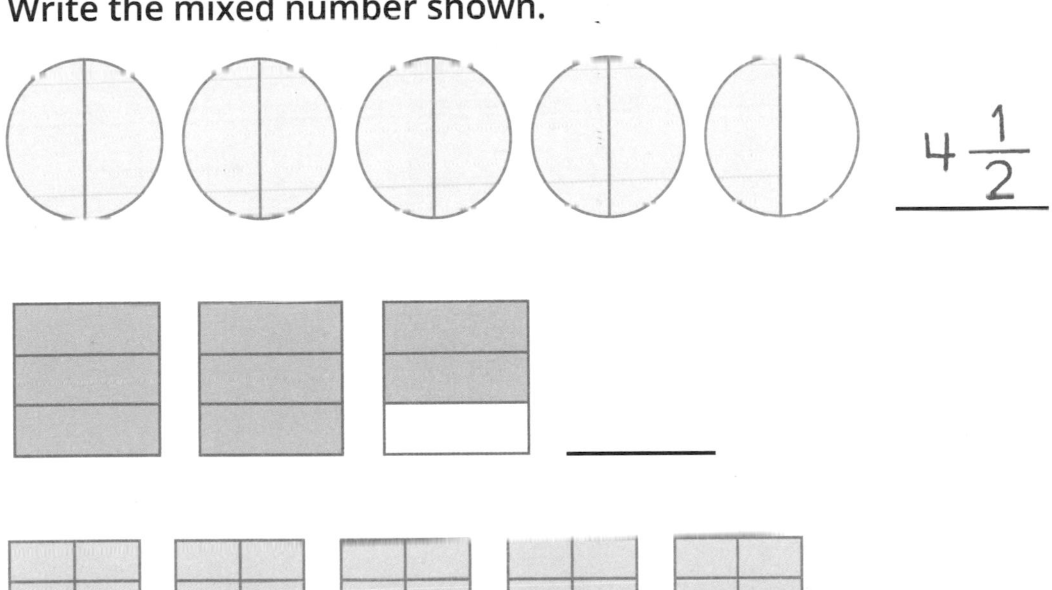

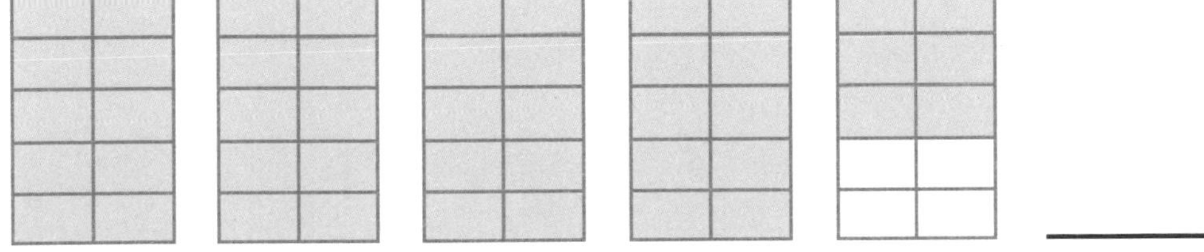

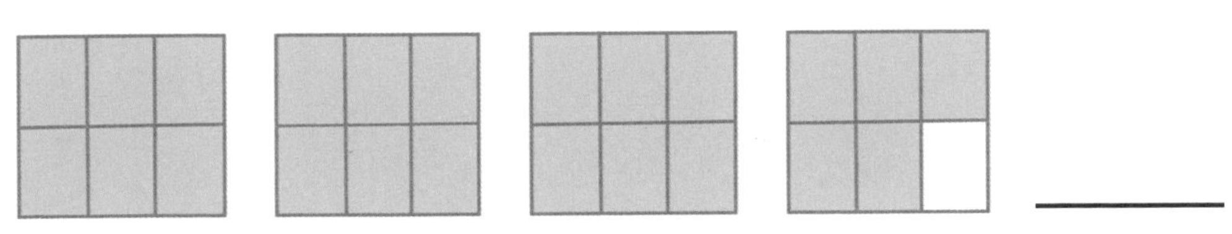

IXL.com
skill ID
UX6

Mixed numbers

Write the mixed number shown.

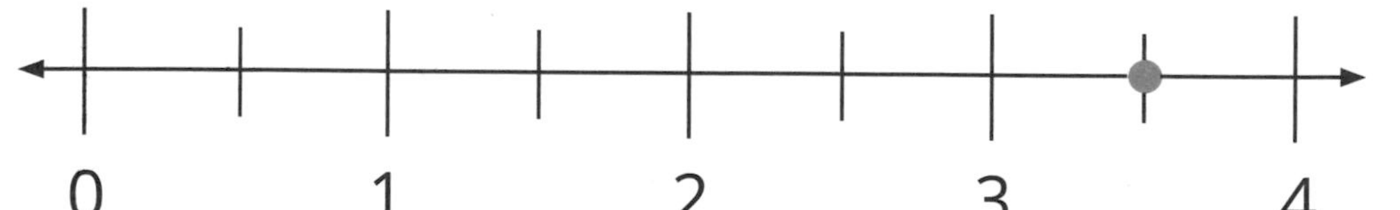

$3\frac{1}{2}$ ______

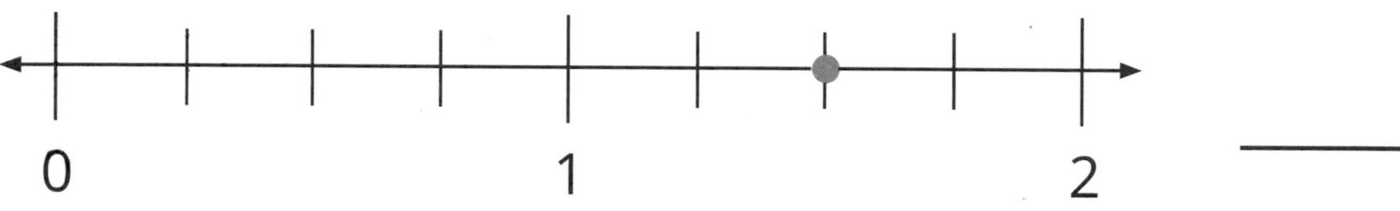

______

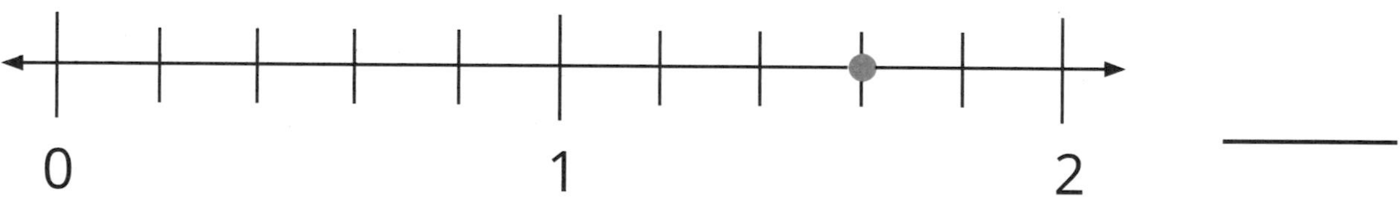

______

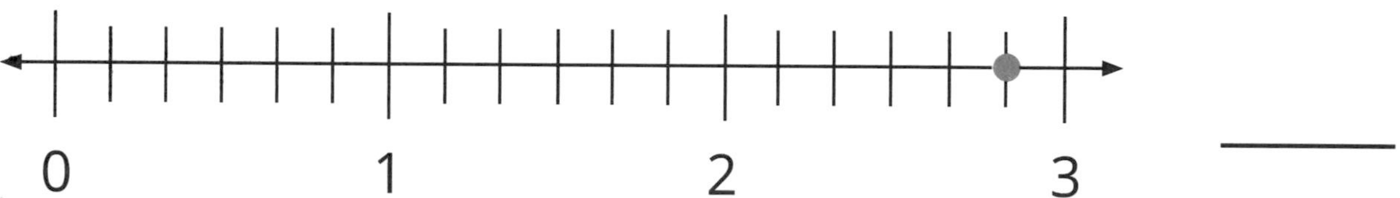

______

Draw a picture that shows each mixed number.

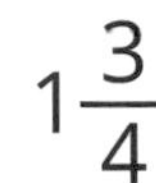

$1\frac{3}{4}$

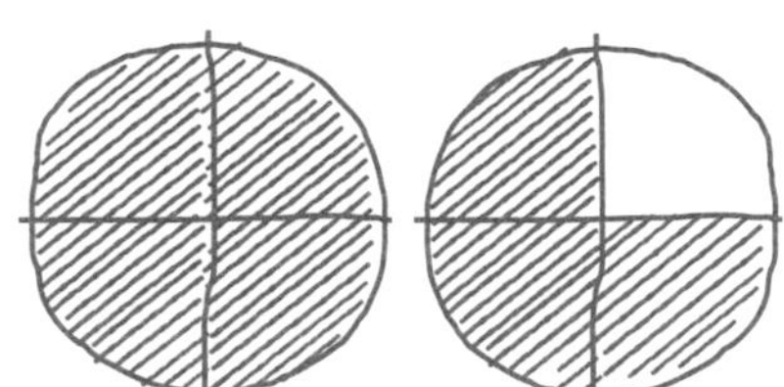

$1\frac{1}{2}$

$3\frac{1}{6}$

$2\frac{2}{4}$

Show each mixed number on a number line.

$2\frac{4}{5}$

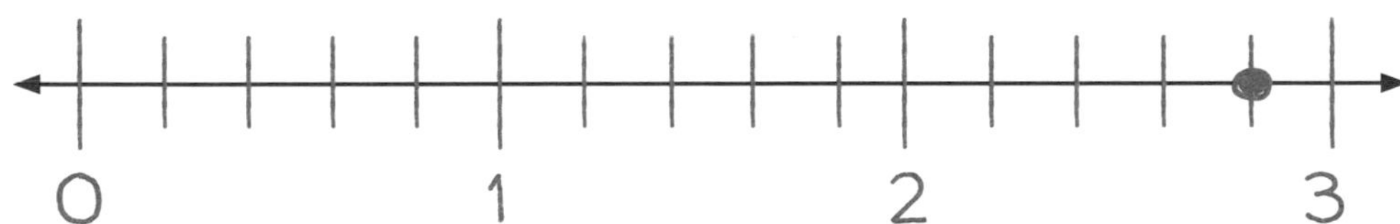

$3\frac{1}{3}$

$1\frac{3}{4}$

Improper fractions

Let's Learn!

You can also use **improper fractions** to show fractions that are greater than 1. Improper fractions are fractions whose numerators are larger than their denominators.

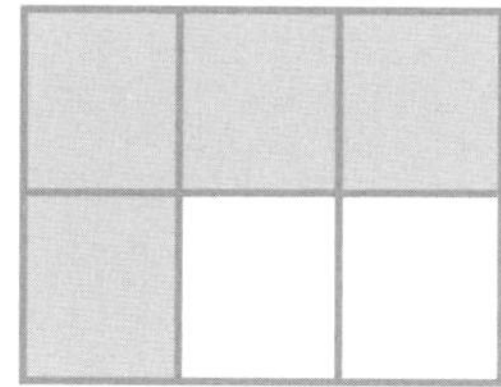

$\frac{10}{6}$ ← number of shaded parts / number of equal parts per whole

Write each improper fraction.

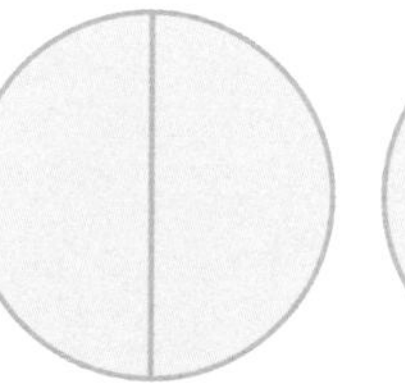

$\frac{7}{2}$

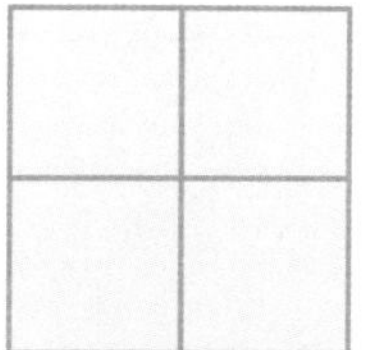
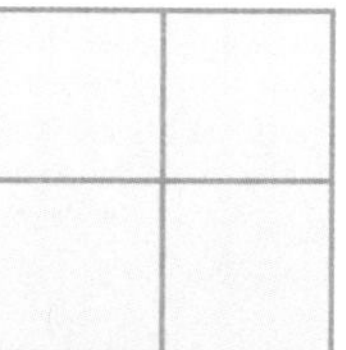
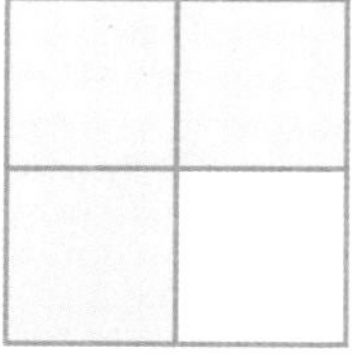

______

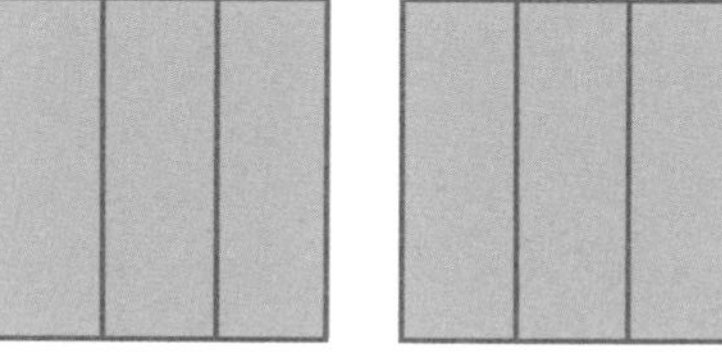

______

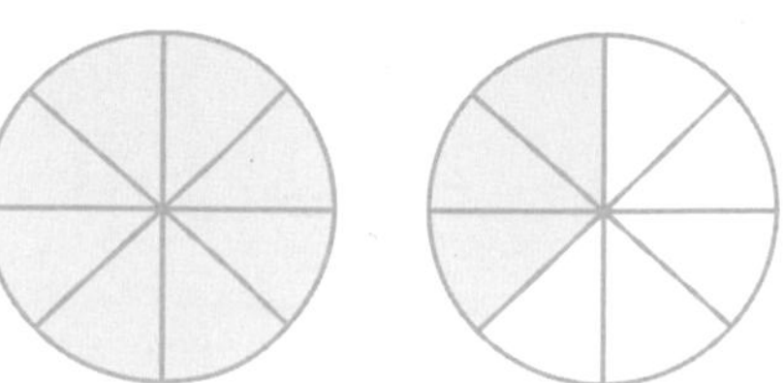

______

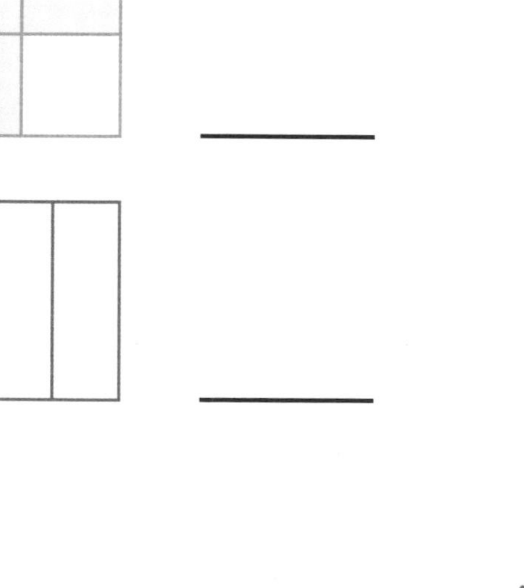

Let's Learn!

You can write improper fractions as mixed numbers to represent the same amount.

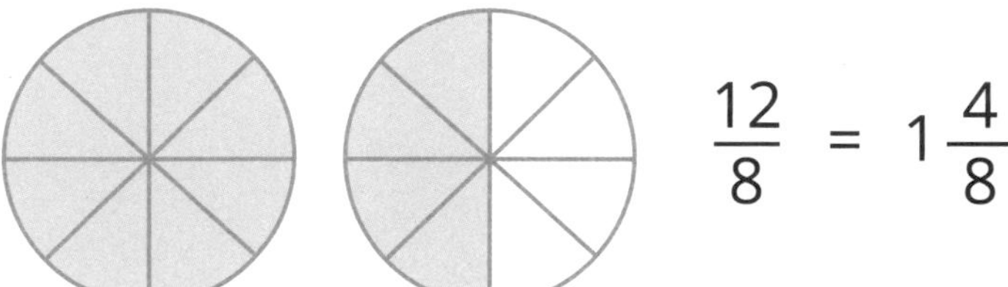

$$\frac{12}{8} = 1\frac{4}{8}$$

Write each improper fraction as a mixed number or a whole number.

$\frac{7}{4}$ = $1\frac{3}{4}$

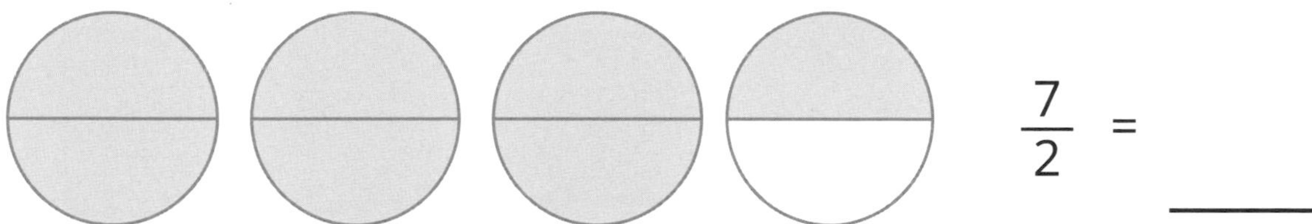

$\frac{7}{2}$ = ______

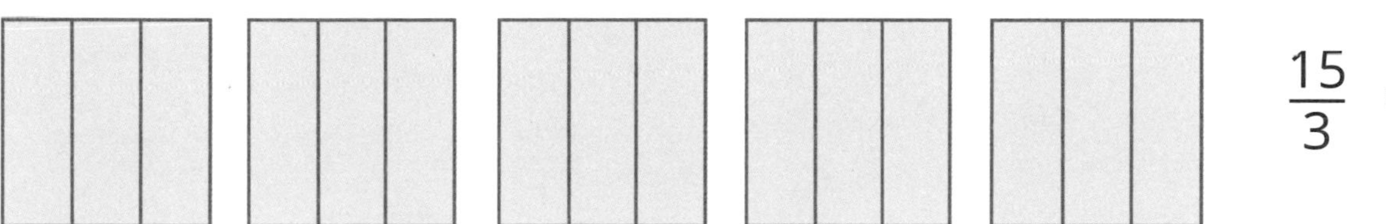

$\frac{15}{3}$ = ______

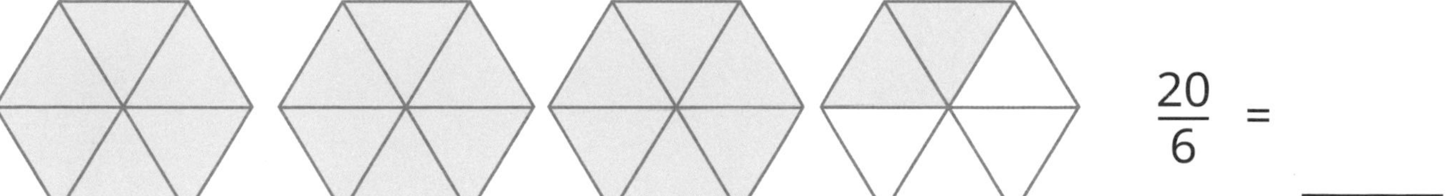

$\frac{20}{6}$ = ______

Mixed numbers and improper fractions

Write each improper fraction as a mixed number.

$\frac{14}{4} =$ $3\frac{2}{4}$

$\frac{10}{3} =$ ______

$\frac{41}{9} =$ ______

$\frac{23}{12} =$ ______

$\frac{31}{11} =$ ______

$\frac{40}{7} =$ ______

Write each mixed number as an improper fraction.

$4\frac{1}{2} =$ $\frac{9}{2}$

$5\frac{1}{4} =$ ______

$3\frac{4}{10} =$ ______

$5\frac{7}{8} =$ ______

$6\frac{4}{7} =$ ______

$7\frac{5}{11} =$ ______

IXL.com
skill ID
JFE

Match the equal numbers.

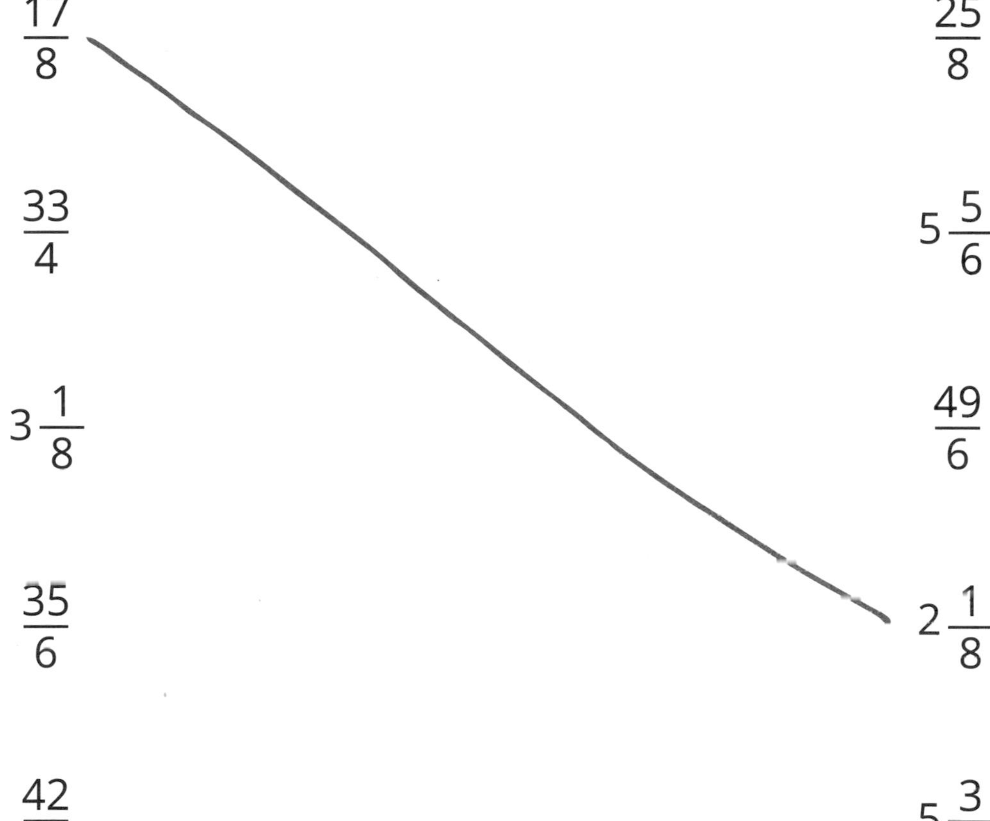

$\frac{17}{8}$	$\frac{25}{8}$
$\frac{33}{4}$	$5\frac{5}{6}$
$3\frac{1}{8}$	$\frac{49}{6}$
$\frac{35}{6}$	$2\frac{1}{8}$
$\frac{42}{8}$	$5\frac{3}{4}$
$8\frac{1}{6}$	$5\frac{2}{8}$
$\frac{23}{4}$	$\frac{50}{8}$
$6\frac{2}{8}$	$8\frac{1}{4}$

Answer each question. Draw a picture to help!

You need to measure out $2\frac{1}{4}$ cups of flour for a pretzel recipe. You are using a $\frac{1}{4}$-cup scoop. How many scoops of flour will you need?

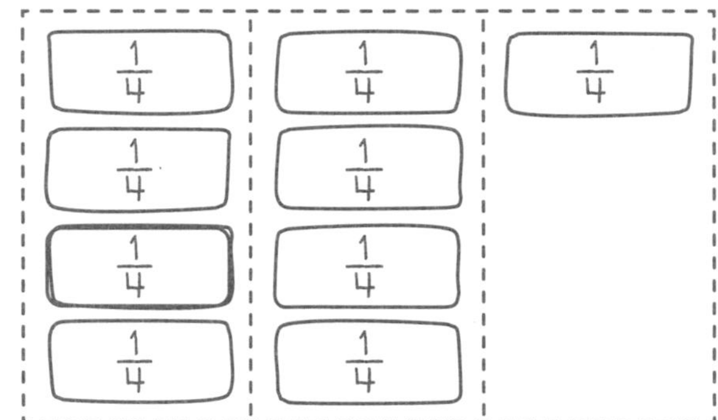

9 SCOOPS

Molly's pitcher holds $5\frac{1}{2}$ cups of juice. She is pouring juice into glasses that can hold $\frac{1}{2}$ of a cup of juice. How many cups can she fill with one pitcher?

____

One lap of a track is $\frac{1}{4}$ of a mile long. If you want to run $3\frac{3}{4}$ miles, how many laps do you need to run?

____

Adding mixed numbers

Let's Learn!

You can add mixed numbers by adding the whole number parts and then adding the fraction parts. Try it with $1\frac{3}{5} + 2\frac{1}{5}$.

Add the whole number parts: 1 + 2 = 3.

Add the fraction parts: $\frac{3}{5} + \frac{1}{5} = \frac{4}{5}$. Then put them together.

$$1\frac{3}{5} \quad + \quad 2\frac{1}{5} \quad = \quad 3\frac{4}{5}$$

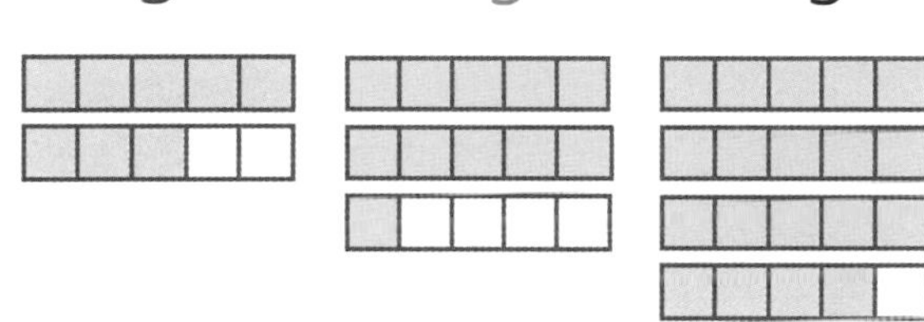

Add.

$2\frac{1}{4} + 4\frac{2}{4} =$ $6\frac{3}{4}$

$3\frac{1}{3} + 1\frac{1}{3} =$ ________

$2\frac{3}{6} + 2\frac{1}{6} =$ ________

$3\frac{3}{8} + 4\frac{4}{8} =$ ________

$4\frac{1}{5} + 2\frac{2}{5} =$ ________

$6\frac{1}{9} + 3\frac{4}{9} =$ ________

Adding mixed numbers with regrouping

Let's Learn!

When you add mixed numbers, the fraction part may become larger than a whole. For example, when you add $1\frac{2}{3} + 2\frac{2}{3}$, you get $3\frac{4}{3}$. Since $\frac{4}{3}$ is larger than a whole, you can regroup.

$$3\frac{4}{3} = 4\frac{1}{3}$$

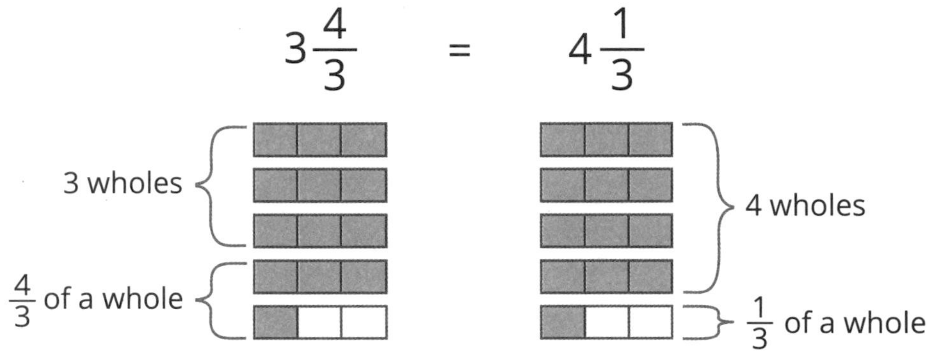

So, $1\frac{2}{3} + 2\frac{2}{3} = 4\frac{1}{3}$.

Add. Regroup the sum.

$2\frac{3}{5} + 1\frac{4}{5} =$ $4\frac{2}{5}$

$3\frac{5}{6} + 1\frac{3}{6} =$ ______

$5\frac{7}{8} + 3\frac{7}{8} =$ ______

$4\frac{3}{6} + 2\frac{4}{6} =$ ______

$3\frac{4}{5} + 5\frac{4}{5} =$ ______

$1\frac{3}{9} + 4\frac{7}{9} =$ ______

Add. Regroup the sum, if necessary.

$1\frac{2}{7} + 2\frac{3}{7} =$ $3\frac{5}{7}$

$2\frac{3}{8} + 4\frac{1}{8} =$ ______

$1\frac{2}{4} + 2\frac{1}{4} =$ ______

$5\frac{3}{6} + 1\frac{1}{6} =$ ______

$6\frac{1}{5} + 3\frac{3}{5} =$ ______

$6\frac{2}{10} + 8\frac{5}{10} =$ ______

$3\frac{3}{4} + 2\frac{2}{4} =$ ______

$5\frac{5}{6} + 2\frac{2}{6} =$ ______

$7\frac{4}{8} + 2\frac{4}{8} =$ ______

$2\frac{8}{9} + 4\frac{7}{9} =$ ______

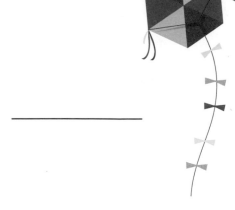

Answer each question. Regroup the sum, if necessary.

In June, Grace planted a sunflower that was $1\frac{3}{12}$ feet tall. By August, the sunflower had grown $5\frac{7}{12}$ feet taller. How tall was the sunflower in August? ____________

Mike is making a big pot of soup for a family dinner. He needs $3\frac{3}{4}$ cups of vegetable broth and $1\frac{1}{4}$ cups of water. How many cups of liquid is that in all? ____________

Mrs. Fina's class painted a mural on the hallway wall. One group painted a section that was $5\frac{3}{4}$ meters long. Another group painted a section that was $6\frac{2}{4}$ meters long. How long is the mural? ____________

Mark ran $2\frac{6}{10}$ miles at cross-country practice on Monday. At Wednesday's practice, Mark ran $3\frac{5}{10}$ miles. How far did Mark run in all? ____________

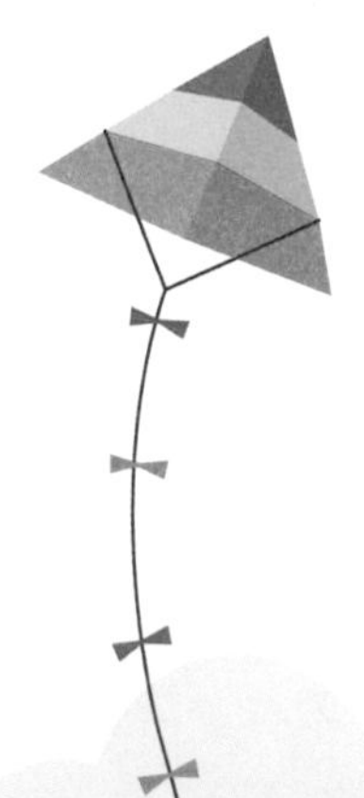

Subtracting mixed numbers

Let's Learn!

You can subtract mixed numbers by subtracting the whole number parts and then subtracting the fraction parts. Try it with $4\frac{2}{3} - 1\frac{1}{3}$.

Subtract the whole number parts: 4 – 1 = 3.

Subtract the fraction parts: $\frac{2}{3} - \frac{1}{3} = \frac{1}{3}$. Then put them together.

$$4\frac{2}{3} - 1\frac{1}{3} = 3\frac{1}{3}$$

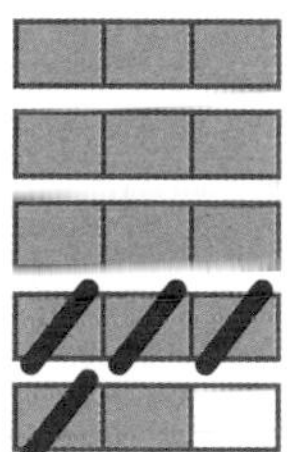

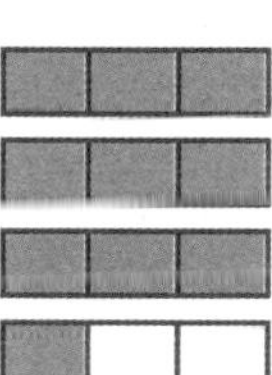

Subtract.

$3\frac{3}{4} - 2\frac{2}{4} =$ $1\frac{1}{4}$

$4\frac{2}{3} - 2\frac{1}{3} =$ ______

$3\frac{4}{5} - 2\frac{1}{5} =$ ______

$4\frac{5}{6} - 1\frac{3}{6} =$ ______

$5\frac{5}{8} - 2\frac{4}{8} =$ ______

$4\frac{5}{7} - 1\frac{3}{7} =$ ______

62 Subtracting mixed numbers with regrouping

Let's Learn!

Sometimes when you subtract mixed numbers, the first fraction part is smaller than the second fraction part, and you can't subtract them. For example, with $4\frac{1}{4} - 1\frac{3}{4}$, you can't subtract $\frac{1}{4} - \frac{3}{4}$.

So, regroup! You can rewrite $4\frac{1}{4}$ as $3\frac{5}{4}$.

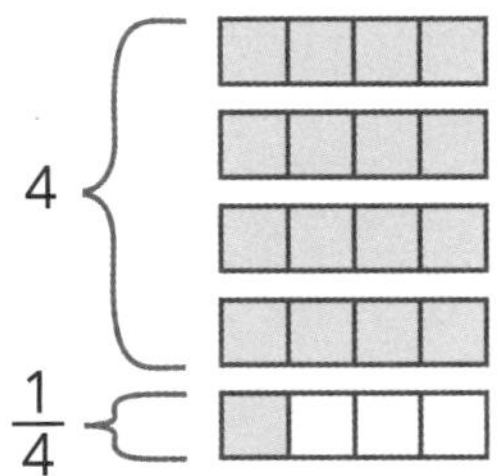

Rewrite the problem and solve.

$$3\frac{5}{4} - 1\frac{3}{4} = 2\frac{2}{4}$$

Regroup. Then subtract.

$2\frac{4}{3}$ ~~$3\frac{1}{3}$~~ $- 1\frac{2}{3} =$ $1\frac{2}{3}$

$5\frac{1}{5} - 3\frac{4}{5} =$ ______

$5\frac{3}{6} - 2\frac{4}{6} =$ ______

$7\frac{2}{8} - 4\frac{5}{8} =$ ______

Subtract. Regroup, if necessary.

$3\frac{7}{8} - 1\frac{5}{8} =$ $2\frac{2}{8}$

$5\frac{6}{9} - 2\frac{2}{9} =$ ______

$8\frac{3}{5} - 5\frac{2}{5} =$ ______

$6\frac{5}{6} - 2\frac{3}{6} =$ ______

$7\frac{9}{10} - 2\frac{7}{10} =$ ______

$9\frac{8}{12} - 2\frac{6}{12} =$ ______

$7\frac{1}{4} - 2\frac{2}{4} =$ ______

$3\frac{1}{6} - 1\frac{2}{6} =$ ______

$4\frac{6}{9} - 1\frac{8}{9} =$ ______

$9\frac{3}{11} - 4\frac{5}{11} =$ ______

Adding and subtracting mixed numbers

Add or subtract. Regroup, if necessary.

$3\frac{1}{6} + 2\frac{2}{6} =$ ______

$5\frac{2}{5} - 2\frac{1}{5} =$ ______

$6\frac{5}{8} - 2\frac{3}{8} =$ ______

$2\frac{2}{7} + 2\frac{4}{7} =$ ______

$3 + 2\frac{1}{2} =$ ______

$3\frac{4}{10} - 2\frac{2}{10} =$ ______

$7\frac{9}{12} - 5\frac{2}{12} =$ ______

$1\frac{2}{5} + 2\frac{2}{5} =$ ______

$3 + 3\frac{1}{4} =$ ______

$2\frac{3}{5} + 1\frac{2}{5} =$ ______

$7 + 3\frac{5}{8} =$ ______

$4 - 2\frac{1}{2} =$ ______

$8\frac{5}{9} - 2\frac{7}{9} =$ ______

Match each problem with its answer.

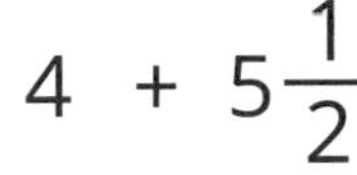

$4 + 5\frac{1}{2}$	$7\frac{2}{4}$
$9\frac{3}{4} - 2\frac{1}{4}$	9
$9\frac{5}{6} - 1\frac{4}{6}$	$8\frac{1}{4}$
$4\frac{1}{2} + 4\frac{1}{2}$	$6\frac{3}{6}$
$3\frac{4}{6} + 3\frac{5}{6}$	$7\frac{3}{4}$
$4\frac{2}{4} + 3\frac{3}{4}$	$9\frac{1}{2}$
$10\frac{2}{6} - 3\frac{5}{6}$	$6\frac{5}{6}$
$9\frac{1}{4} - 1\frac{2}{4}$	$7\frac{3}{6}$
$8\frac{1}{6} - 1\frac{2}{6}$	$8\frac{1}{6}$

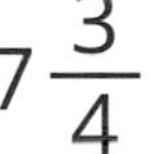

Word problems

Answer each question.

Jimmy's ski lesson is $2\frac{1}{4}$ hours long. After his lesson, he skis on his own for another $1\frac{2}{4}$ hours. How many hours does Jimmy spend skiing?

____

Hailey is making chicken salad. She needs $2\frac{2}{3}$ tablespoons of olive oil for the chicken and $3\frac{1}{3}$ tablespoons of olive oil for the salad dressing. How much olive oil does Hailey need in all?

____

A car's gas tank had $9\frac{3}{8}$ gallons of gas. After driving 100 miles, the gas tank had $5\frac{7}{8}$ gallons remaining. How much gas was used?

____

Becca bought curtains that were $9\frac{6}{12}$ feet long, but they were too big for her windows. She cut them to be $2\frac{7}{12}$ feet shorter. How long are the curtains now?

____

Let's Learn!

You can write fractions as sums of unit fractions. For example, $\frac{3}{8} = \frac{1}{8} + \frac{1}{8} + \frac{1}{8}$. Remember that repeated addition is the same as multiplication. So, $\frac{1}{8} + \frac{1}{8} + \frac{1}{8}$ is the same as $3 \times \frac{1}{8}$!

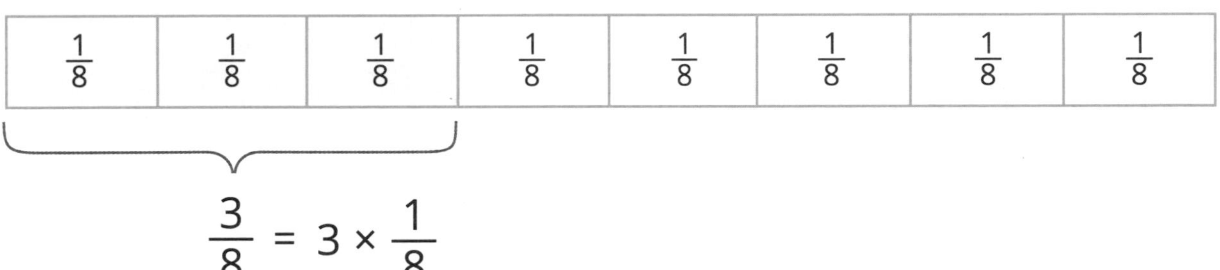

$$\frac{3}{8} = 3 \times \frac{1}{8}$$

Write each fraction as a multiple of a unit fraction.

$\frac{1}{3}$	$\frac{1}{3}$	$\frac{1}{3}$

$\frac{2}{3} = 2 \times \frac{1}{3}$

$\frac{1}{4}$	$\frac{1}{4}$	$\frac{1}{4}$	$\frac{1}{4}$

$\frac{3}{4} =$ ________

$\frac{1}{5}$	$\frac{1}{5}$	$\frac{1}{5}$	$\frac{1}{5}$	$\frac{1}{5}$

$\frac{3}{5} =$ ________

$\frac{1}{6}$	$\frac{1}{6}$	$\frac{1}{6}$	$\frac{1}{6}$	$\frac{1}{6}$	$\frac{1}{6}$

$\frac{5}{6} =$ ________

$\frac{1}{8}$	$\frac{1}{8}$	$\frac{1}{8}$	$\frac{1}{8}$	$\frac{1}{8}$	$\frac{1}{8}$	$\frac{1}{8}$	$\frac{1}{8}$

$\frac{7}{8} =$ ________

$\frac{1}{9}$	$\frac{1}{9}$	$\frac{1}{9}$	$\frac{1}{9}$	$\frac{1}{9}$	$\frac{1}{9}$	$\frac{1}{9}$	$\frac{1}{9}$	$\frac{1}{9}$

$\frac{7}{9} =$ ________

For more practice, visit IXL.com or the IXL mobile app and enter this code in the search bar.

IXL.com skill ID **8J3**

Multiplying fractions

Write each fraction as a multiple of a unit fraction.

$\frac{3}{10}$ = ____________________

$\frac{2}{6}$ = ____________________

$\frac{4}{5}$ = ____________________

$\frac{8}{12}$ = ____________________

$\frac{9}{10}$ = ____________________

$\frac{5}{9}$ = ____________________

$\frac{5}{8}$ = ____________________

$\frac{6}{11}$ = ____________________

$\frac{3}{7}$ = ____________________

$\frac{7}{12}$ = ____________________

IXL.com skill ID VYG

Let's Learn!

You can multiply any fraction by a whole number. When you multiply $3 \times \frac{2}{8}$, you are adding $\frac{2}{8}$ three times.

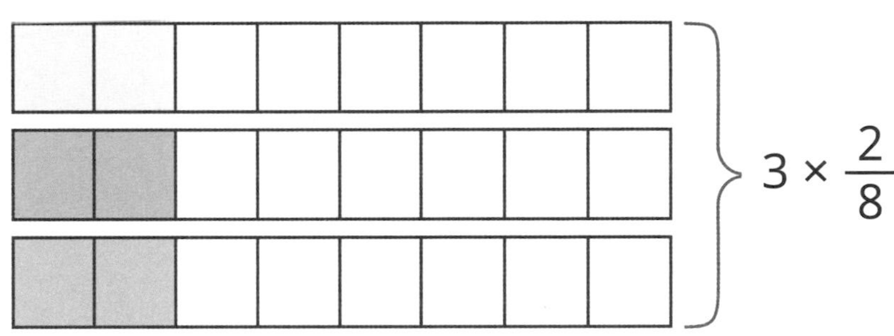

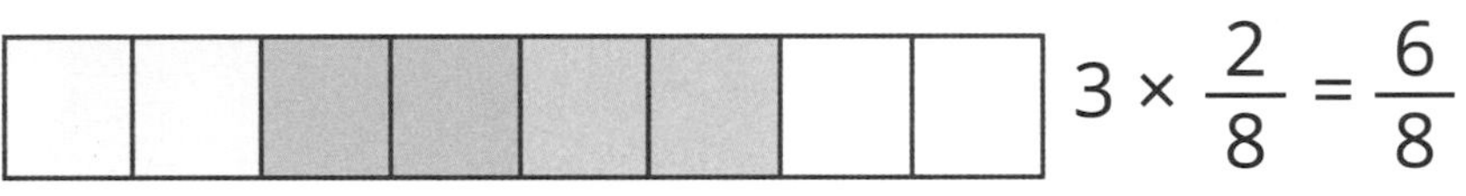

Write the addition and multiplication equations for each model.

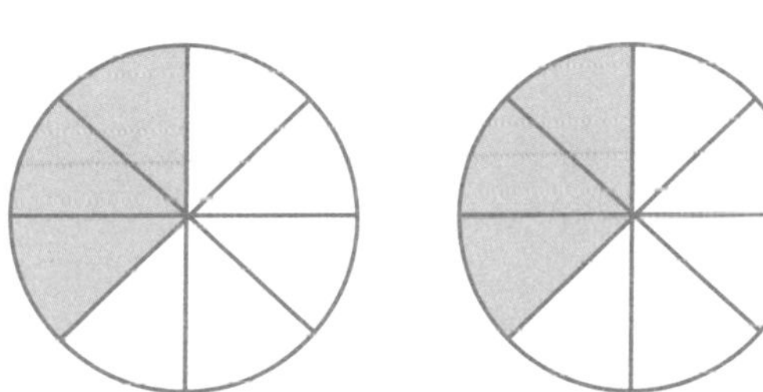

$\frac{3}{8}$ + $\frac{3}{8}$ = $\frac{6}{8}$

2 × $\frac{3}{8}$ = $\frac{6}{8}$

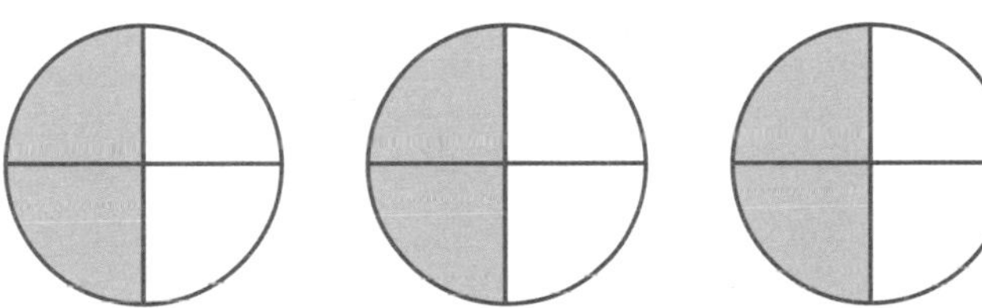

_____ + _____ + _____ = _____

_____ × _____ = _____

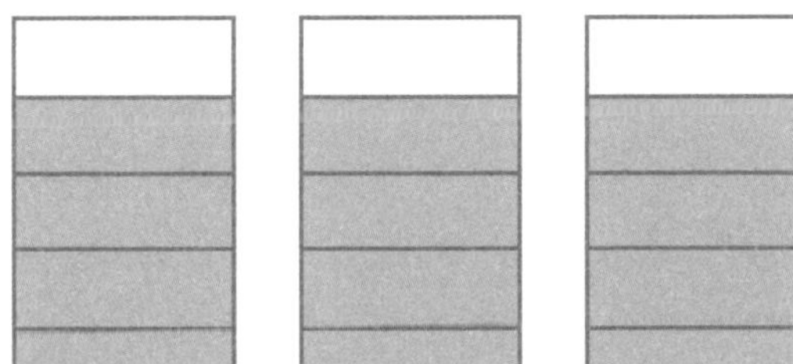

_____ + _____ + _____ = _____

_____ × _____ = _____

Multiplying fractions

Write the multiplication equation for each model.

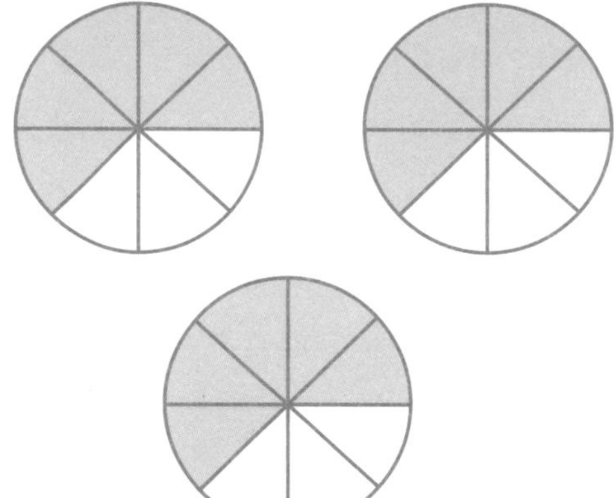

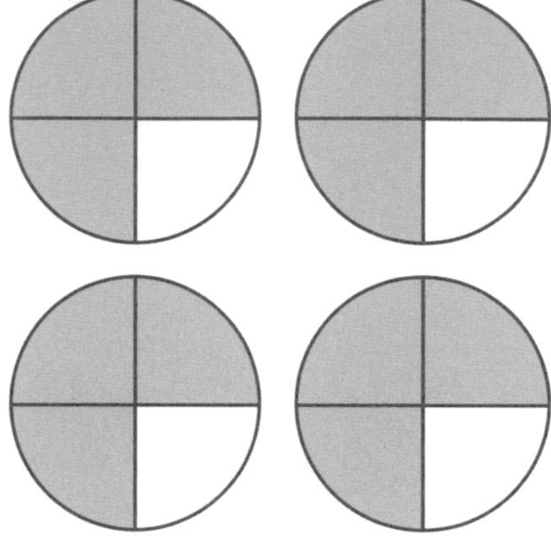

_______ × ________ = _______

_______ × ________ = _______

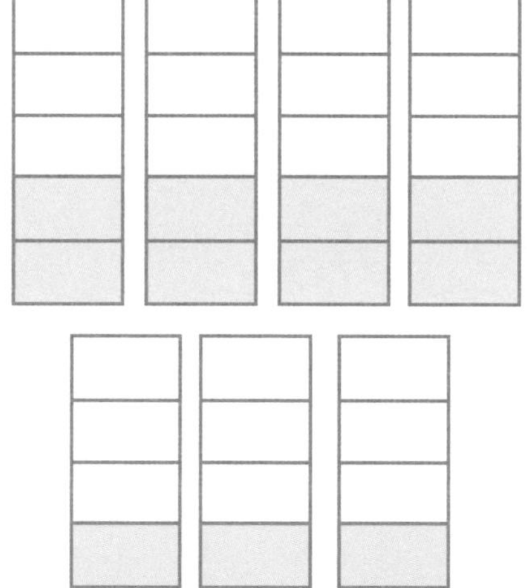

_______ × ________ = _______

_______ × ________ = _______

IXL.com
skill ID
Y5C

Let's Learn!

To multiply a fraction by a whole number, multiply the numerator by the whole number. Keep the denominator the same.

$$5 \times \frac{3}{8} = \frac{5 \times 3}{8} = \frac{15}{8}$$

Multiply.

$4 \times \frac{2}{9} =$ $\frac{8}{9}$

$2 \times \frac{3}{5} =$ ________

$3 \times \frac{6}{11} =$ ________

$5 \times \frac{8}{12} =$ ________

$6 \times \frac{9}{10} =$ ________

$8 \times \frac{6}{7} =$ ________

$7 \times \frac{5}{8} =$ ________

$9 \times \frac{11}{12} =$ ________

CHALLENGE YOURSELF! Write each answer as a mixed number in simplest form.

A THIRD OF A HALF?

You can have a fraction of a fraction! For example, this model shows $\frac{1}{2}$ split into thirds. As you can see, $\frac{1}{3}$ of $\frac{1}{2}$ is $\frac{1}{6}$!

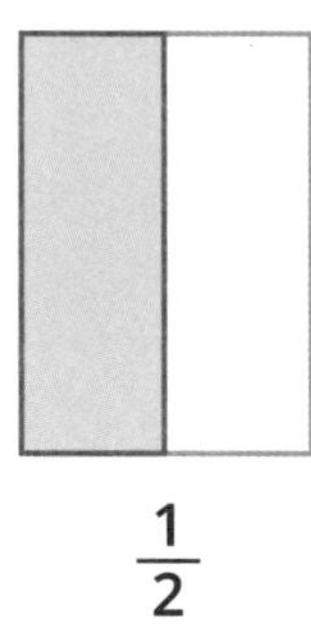

$\frac{1}{2}$

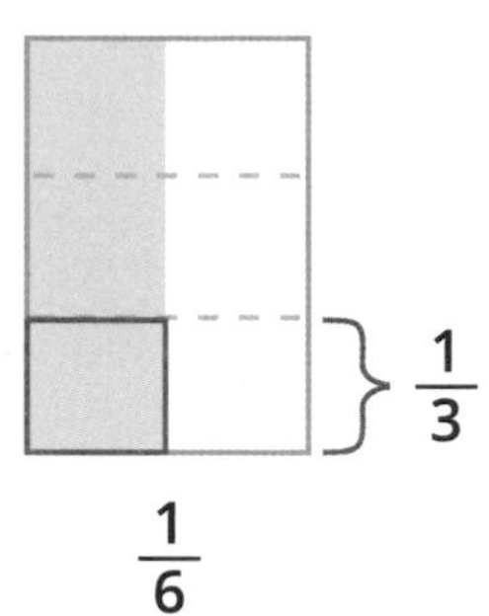

$\frac{1}{6}$

IXL.com skill ID UAY

TRY IT YOURSELF!

Find the fraction of a fraction.

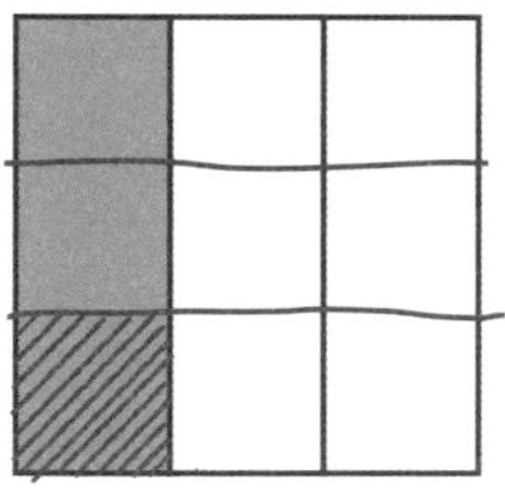

$\frac{1}{3}$ of $\frac{1}{3}$ = $\frac{1}{9}$

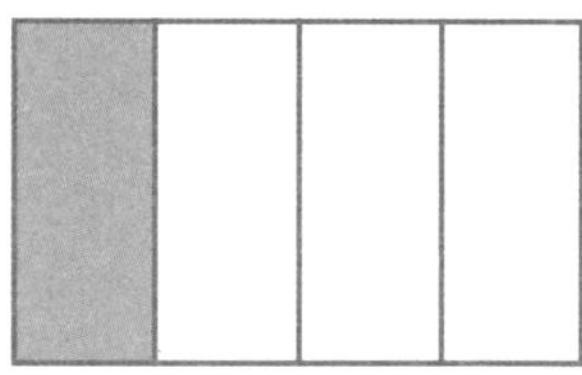

$\frac{1}{2}$ of $\frac{1}{4}$ = ______

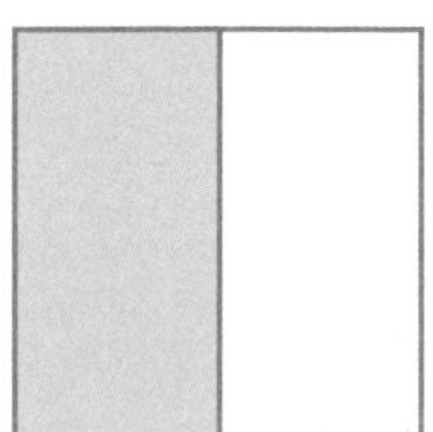

$\frac{1}{5}$ of $\frac{1}{2}$ = ______

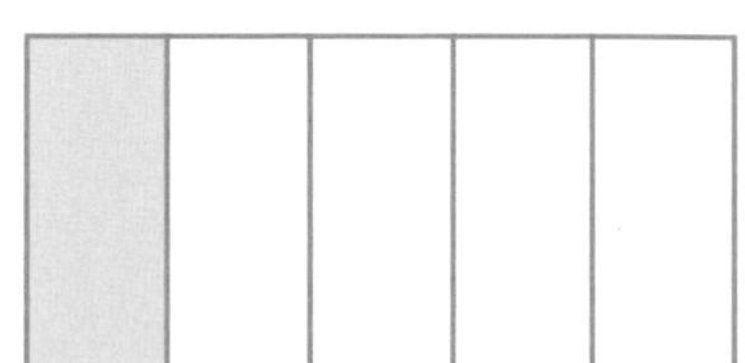

$\frac{1}{4}$ of $\frac{1}{5}$ = ______

MULTIPLY TO FIND A FRACTION OF A FRACTION

If you want to find a fraction of a fraction, you can multiply to get the answer. For example, here is $\frac{2}{3}$ of $\frac{2}{5}$.

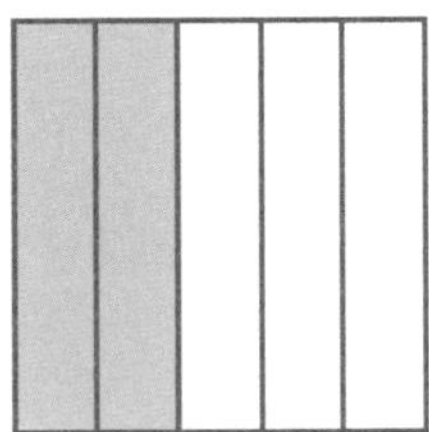

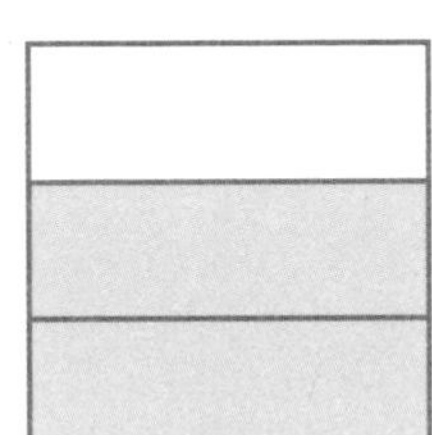

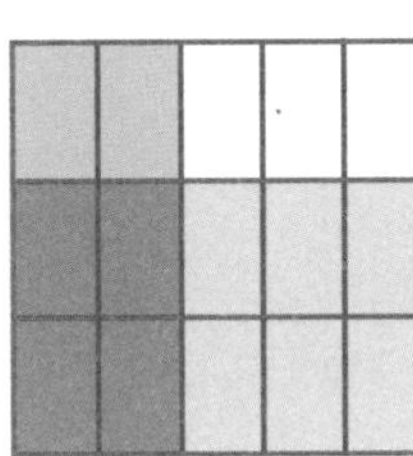

$$\frac{2}{5} \times \frac{2}{3} = \frac{4}{15}$$

To multiply two fractions, multiply the numerators (2 × 2 = 4) and multiply the denominators (5 × 3 = 15).

TRY IT YOURSELF!

IXL.com skill ID **8KV**

Multiply.

$\frac{1}{5} \times \frac{3}{4} = \frac{3}{20}$

$\frac{2}{7} \times \frac{3}{5} =$ ____

$\frac{3}{4} \times \frac{1}{4} =$ ____

$\frac{3}{8} \times \frac{2}{3} =$ ____

$\frac{4}{5} \times \frac{1}{2} =$ ____

$\frac{4}{7} \times \frac{2}{3} =$ ____

Word problems

Answer each question.

There are 5 caterpillars in a row on a stick. Each caterpillar is $\frac{7}{8}$ of an inch long. If the caterpillars line the entire length of the stick, how long is the stick? ______________

Milo makes tacos 4 times each month. He puts $\frac{3}{8}$ of a tablespoon of black pepper in his tacos. How much black pepper does Milo use for tacos in one month? ______________

A bottle of ranch salad dressing weighs $\frac{5}{8}$ of a pound. There are 9 of these bottles on a shelf at the store. How much weight is on the shelf? ______________

Carrie spends $\frac{4}{6}$ of an hour at the gym every day. How much time does she spend at the gym each week? ______________

Graham's violin teacher challenged him to practice for 5 hours in one week. If he practices $\frac{3}{4}$ of an hour each day, will he reach this goal? ______________

Add, subtract, or multiply.

$\frac{5}{8} + \frac{1}{8} =$ ______

$\frac{10}{12} - \frac{4}{12} =$ ______

$2 \times \frac{1}{10} =$ ______

$4 \times \frac{5}{6} =$ ______

$\frac{3}{8} + \frac{3}{8} =$ ______

$\frac{9}{10} - \frac{1}{10} =$ ______

$2\frac{3}{4} - \frac{1}{4} =$ ______

$6 \times \frac{4}{3} =$ ______

$\frac{5}{6} + \frac{3}{6} =$ ______

$2\frac{2}{9} - 1\frac{1}{9} =$ ______

Add, subtract, or multiply. Draw a line between the matching answers.

$\frac{7}{8} - \frac{1}{8} = \frac{6}{8}$

$\frac{2}{12} + \frac{6}{12}$

$\frac{1}{5} + \frac{1}{5}$

$\frac{6}{8} + \frac{6}{8}$

$\frac{2}{10} + \frac{5}{10}$

$\frac{3}{10} + \frac{3}{10}$

$\frac{10}{12} - \frac{1}{12}$

$5 \times \frac{2}{12}$

$\frac{4}{5} - \frac{2}{5}$

$3 \times \frac{2}{10}$

$4 \times \frac{3}{8}$

$7 \times \frac{1}{10}$

$\frac{7}{12} + \frac{3}{12}$

$\frac{4}{12} + \frac{5}{12}$

$3 \times \frac{2}{8} = \frac{6}{8}$

$\frac{10}{12} - \frac{2}{12}$

Answer each question.

Greg bought a pumpkin and some apples at a produce stand. The apples weighed $\frac{5}{8}$ of a pound. The pumpkin weighed 9 times as much as the apples. How much did the pumpkin weigh? ______

At Madison Elementary School, $\frac{3}{10}$ of the students take band, and another $\frac{6}{10}$ of the students take chorus. The band and chorus perform together in the annual spring concert. What fraction of the students at the school perform in the spring concert? ______

Paul lives $\frac{4}{8}$ of a mile closer to the dog park than Jenna. Jenna lives $\frac{7}{8}$ of a mile from the dog park. How far from the dog park does Paul live? ______

Brynn likes to roller-skate around Bear Park. The path around the park is $\frac{3}{4}$ of a mile long. If she skates 8 laps around the park, how many miles has she skated? ______

Mr. Piccolo's class is planning a party. He noticed that $\frac{5}{12}$ of the class volunteered to bring food and $\frac{3}{12}$ of the class volunteered to bring decorations. How much of the class is **not** bringing anything? ______

HALF OF A HALF OF A HALF

You can find a fraction of a fraction of a fraction!
Follow the steps below to see how.

Emma's house is 1 mile from the library.

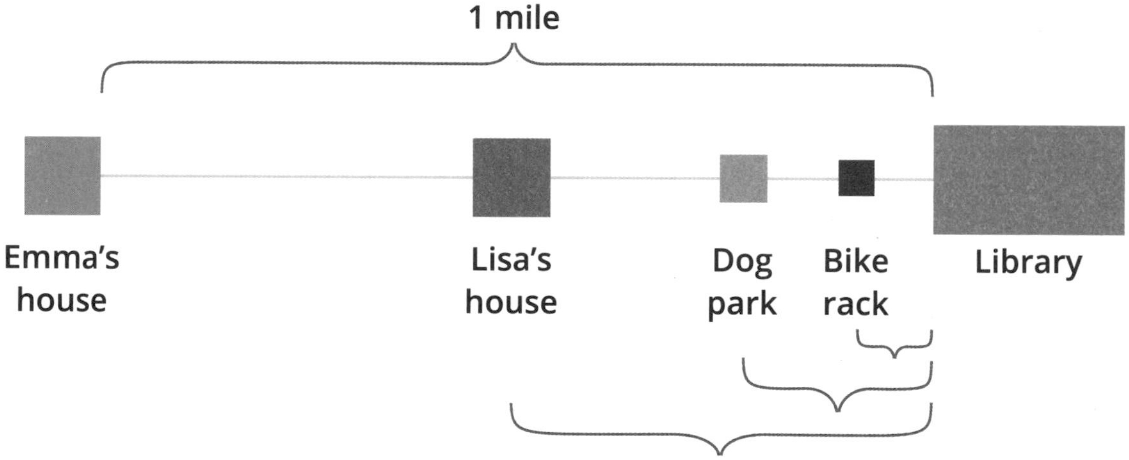

1 mile

Emma's house

Lisa's house

Dog park

Bike rack

Library

Emma's friend Lisa lives exactly halfway between Emma's house and the library. **How far is Lisa's house from the library?** ________________

The dog park is exactly halfway between Lisa's house and the library. **How far is the dog park from the library?** ________________

There is a bike rack exactly halfway between the dog park and the library. **How far is the bike rack from the library?** ________________

Do you see a pattern? If you keep going halfway, what would the next few distances be?

Let's Learn!

Fractions are related to decimals. To get ready for decimals, practice writing fractions that use tenths and hundredths.

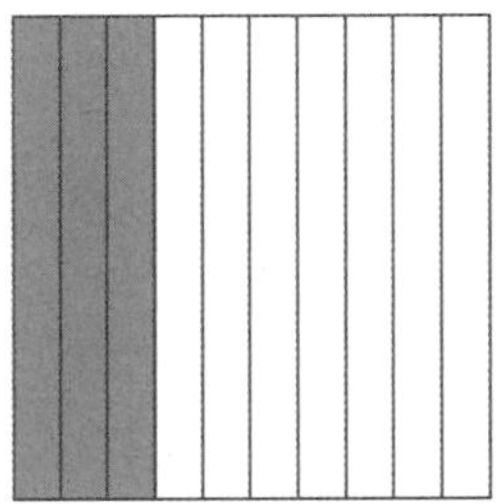

$\frac{3}{10}$

three tenths

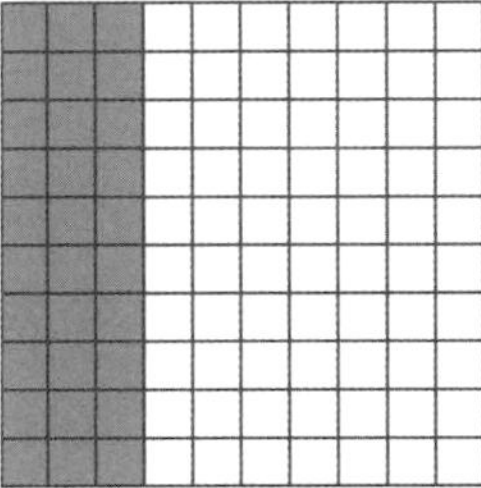

$\frac{30}{100}$

thirty hundredths

Write the fraction shown.

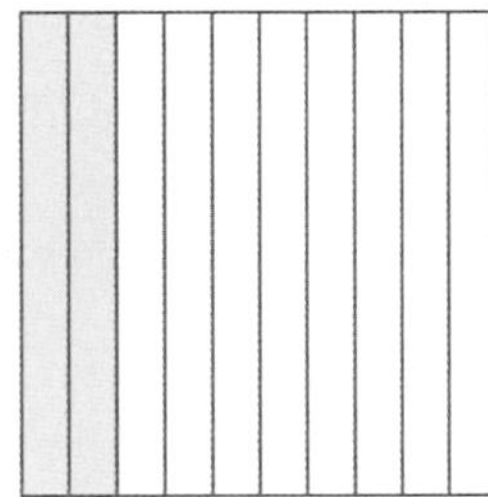

$\frac{2}{10}$

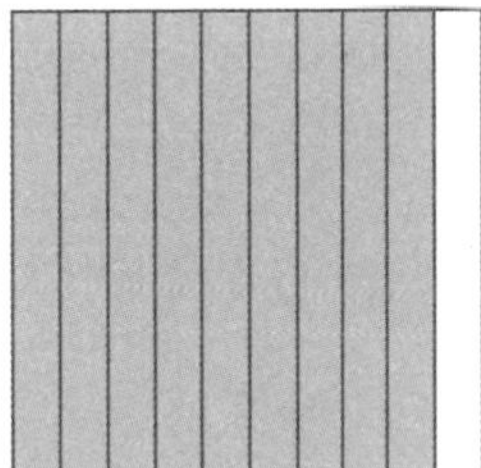

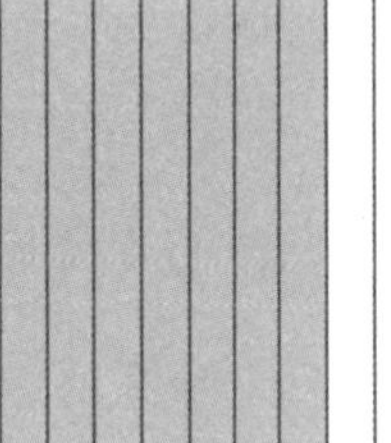

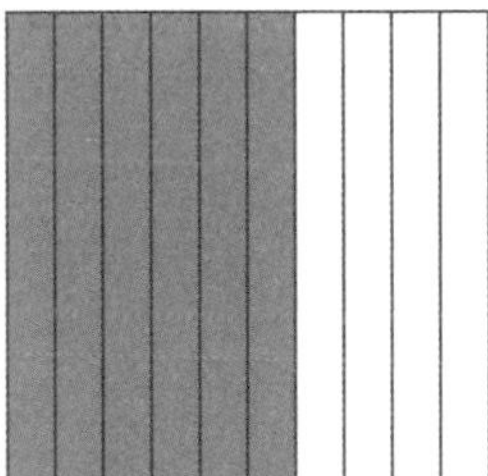

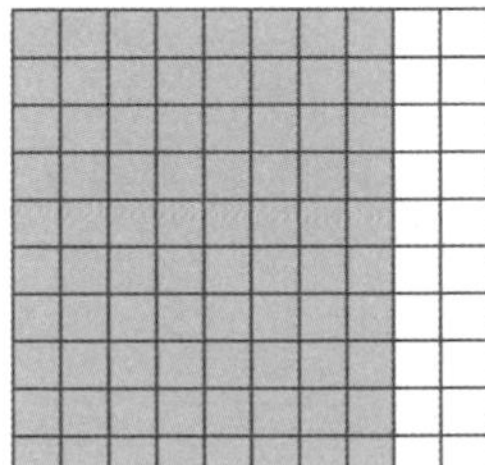

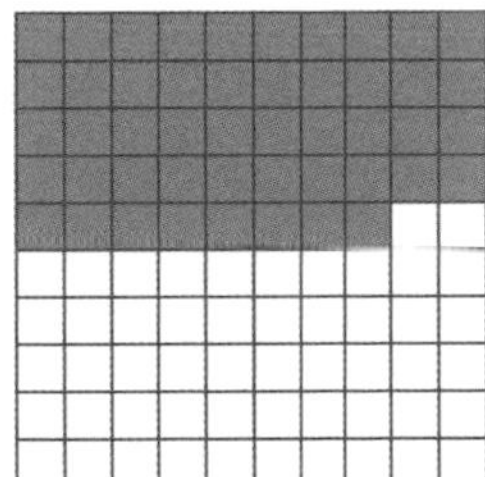

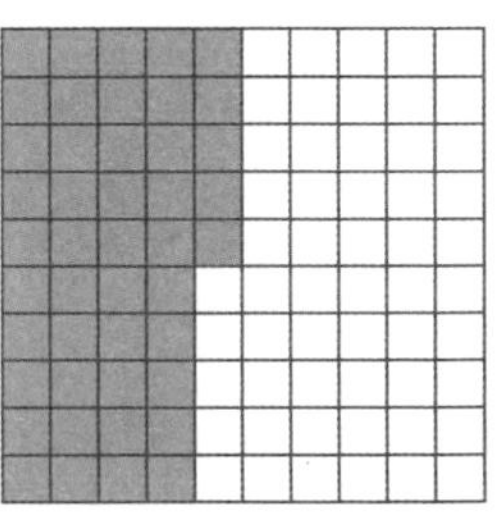

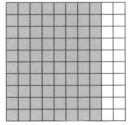

Let's Learn!

Decimals represent parts of wholes, just like fractions! You can use a place value chart to write the decimal. Try it for $\frac{62}{100}$. It is made up of 6 tenths and 2 hundredths.

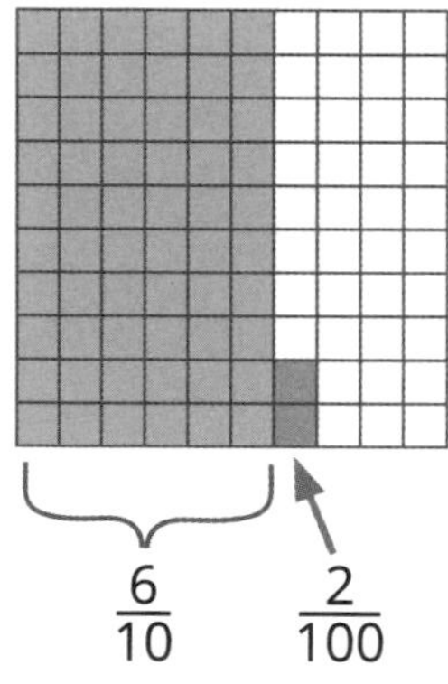

Place Value Chart

Ones		Tenths	Hundredths
0	**.**	**6**	**2**

Write each fraction as a decimal.

$\frac{24}{100}$ = 0.24

$\frac{5}{10}$ = ________

$\frac{13}{100}$ = ________

$\frac{4}{10}$ = ________

$\frac{9}{10}$ = ________

$\frac{64}{100}$ = ________

$\frac{36}{100}$ = ________

$\frac{2}{10}$ = ________

Write each fraction as a decimal.

$1\frac{2}{10}$ = 1.2

$\frac{8}{10}$ = ______

$\frac{30}{100}$ = ______

$\frac{40}{100}$ = ______

$\frac{65}{100}$ = ______

$1\frac{89}{100}$ = ______

$\frac{28}{100}$ = ______

$\frac{4}{100}$ = ______

$\frac{6}{100}$ = ______

$6\frac{5}{100}$ = ______

Write each decimal as a fraction.

0.25 = ______

0.7 = ______

0.91 = ______

0.14 = ______

0.85 = ______

0.02 = ______

Equivalent fractions and decimals

Let's Learn!

Some fractions have denominators that aren't 10 or 100, but you can still write them as decimals! First, find an equivalent fraction with a denominator of 10 or 100. Then you can write the decimal using place value.

$$\frac{7}{20} \xrightarrow{\times 5} \frac{35}{100}$$

$$\frac{7}{20} = \frac{35}{100}$$

Place Value Chart

Ones		Tenths	Hundredths
0	.	3	5

Write each fraction as a decimal.

Fraction	Equivalent Fraction	Decimal
$\frac{3}{5}$	$\frac{6}{10}$	0.6
$\frac{20}{25}$		
$\frac{13}{50}$		
$\frac{39}{50}$		
$\frac{2}{4}$		
$\frac{1}{5}$		

Write each fraction as a decimal.

$\frac{2}{50}$ = 0.04

$\frac{20}{50}$ = ______

$\frac{1}{4}$ = ______

$1\frac{5}{25}$ = ______

$\frac{4}{5}$ = ______

$\frac{1}{2}$ = ______

$5\frac{3}{4}$ = ______

$\frac{35}{50}$ = ______

$\frac{8}{25}$ = ______

$2\frac{16}{20}$ = ______

$\frac{17}{25}$ = ______

$\frac{13}{20}$ = ______

$\frac{49}{50}$ = ______

$3\frac{37}{50}$ = ______

Equivalent fractions and decimals

Match each fraction with its decimal equivalent.

Fraction	Decimal
$\frac{3}{5}$	0.12
$\frac{3}{20}$	0.3
$\frac{6}{50}$	0.6
$\frac{4}{5}$	0.48
$\frac{6}{20}$	0.06
$\frac{33}{50}$	0.15
$\frac{2}{5}$	0.4
$\frac{12}{25}$	0.66
$\frac{3}{50}$	0.8

IXL.com skill ID **6QG**

Write each fraction as a decimal.

Aaron walked $\frac{3}{4}$ of a mile. He walked 0.75 miles.

An apple weighs $\frac{3}{10}$ of a pound. The apple weighs ___________ pounds.

Molly is $10\frac{1}{2}$ years old. She is ___________ years old.

Zoe has $\frac{1}{4}$ of a liter of lemonade. She has ___________ liters of lemonade.

Valerie used $2\frac{1}{5}$ gallons of paint to paint her room. She used ___________ gallons of paint.

Nick's football game lasted $3\frac{1}{2}$ hours. His game was ___________ hours long.

Find the path from point A to point B! Step only on the tiles that are greater than or equal to 0.4 but less than or equal to 0.6.

A ↓

$\frac{5}{10}$	$\frac{10}{25}$	$\frac{4}{10}$	$\frac{2}{20}$	$\frac{3}{50}$
$\frac{30}{50}$	$\frac{20}{25}$	$\frac{1}{25}$	$\frac{17}{20}$	$\frac{2}{10}$
$\frac{2}{5}$	$\frac{43}{100}$	$\frac{8}{20}$	$\frac{19}{25}$	$\frac{13}{20}$
$\frac{4}{5}$	$\frac{2}{25}$	$\frac{15}{25}$	$\frac{19}{20}$	$\frac{7}{50}$
$\frac{4}{50}$	$\frac{6}{20}$	$\frac{49}{100}$	$\frac{61}{100}$	$\frac{7}{10}$
$\frac{3}{5}$	$\frac{59}{100}$	$\frac{9}{20}$	$\frac{4}{20}$	$\frac{31}{50}$

↓ B

Compare each pair of decimals. Fill in each circle with >, <, or =.

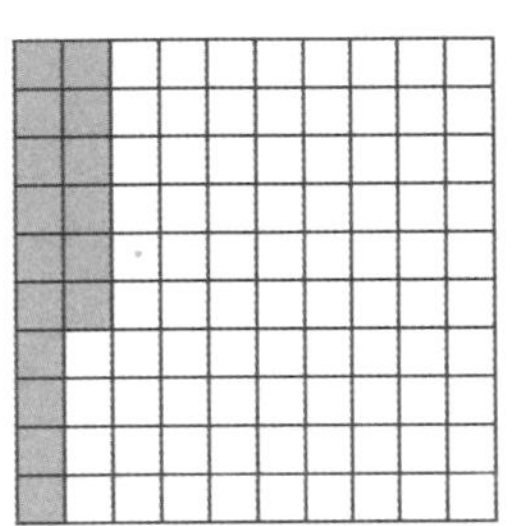 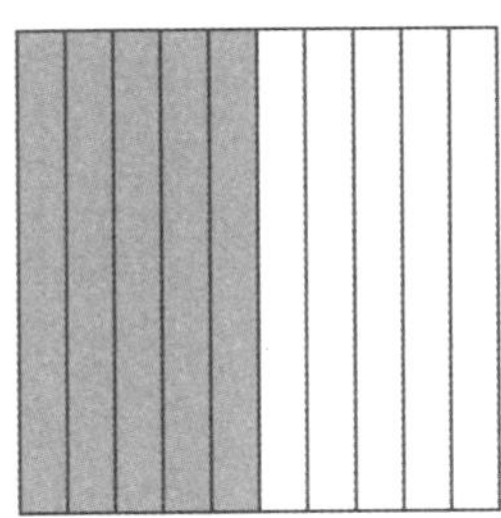

0.16 (<) 0.5

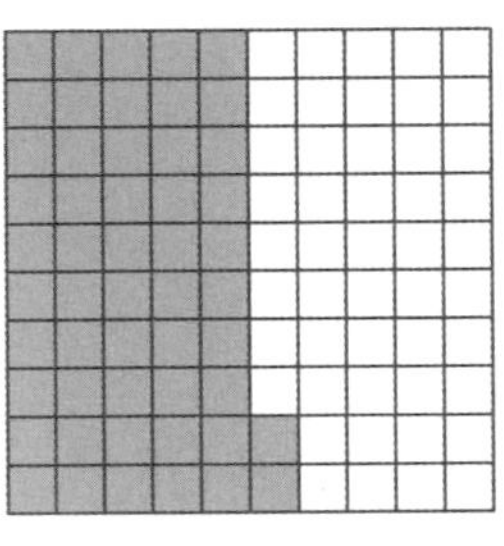 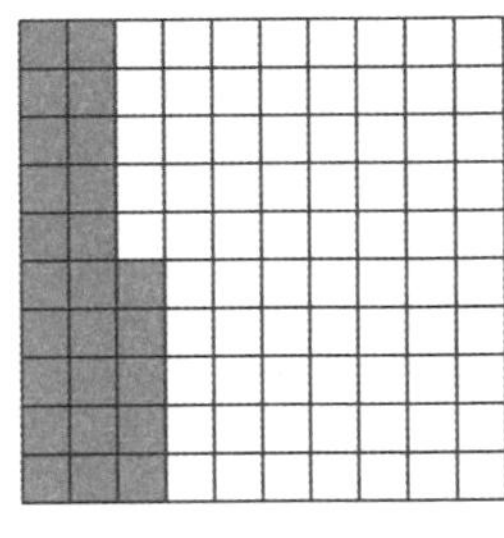

0.52 ◯ 0.25

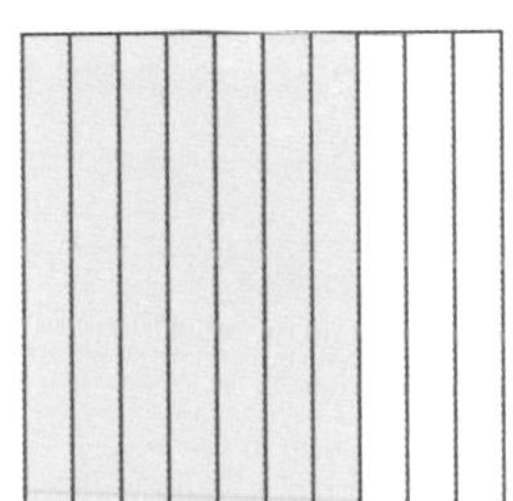 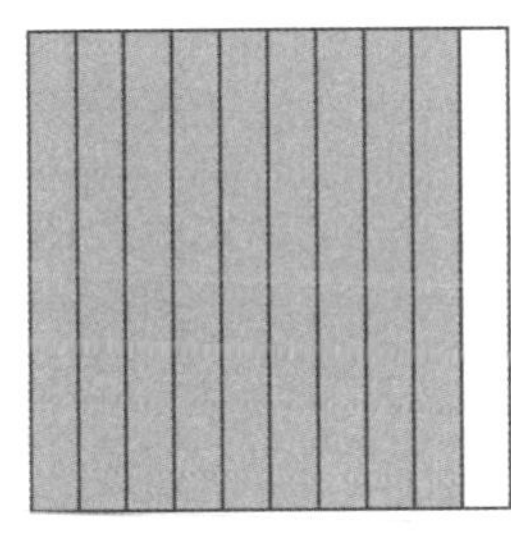

0.7 ◯ 0.9

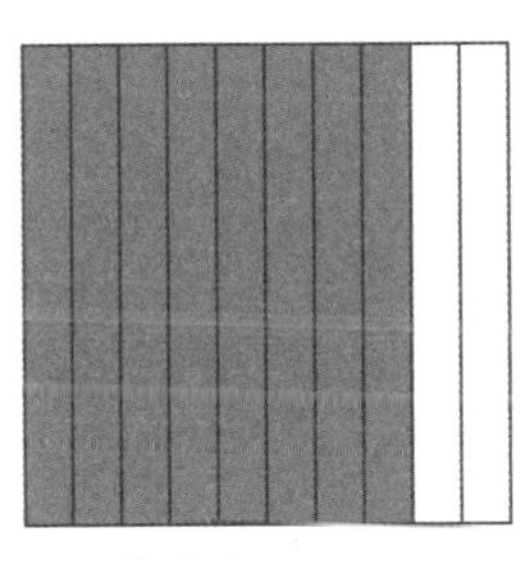 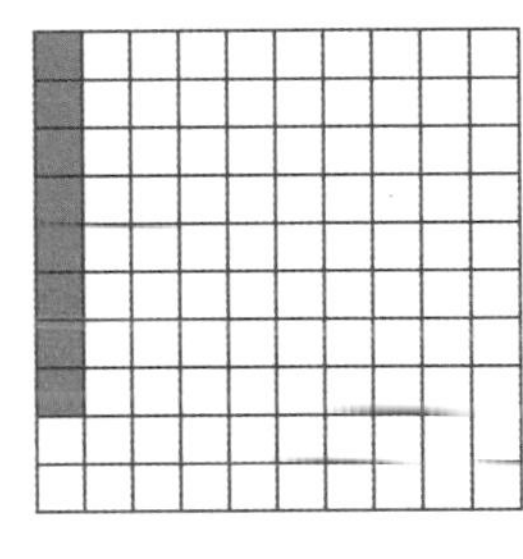

0.8 ◯ 0.08

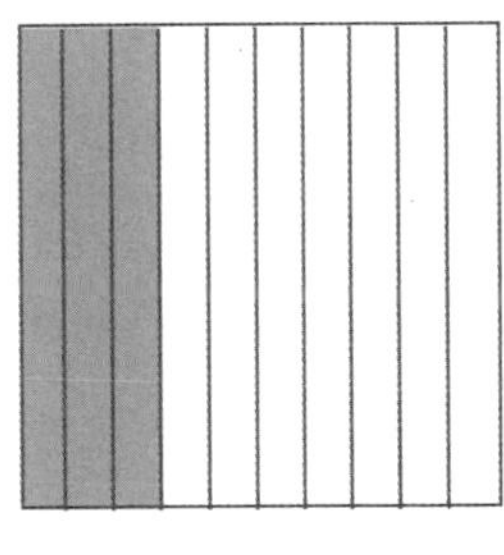 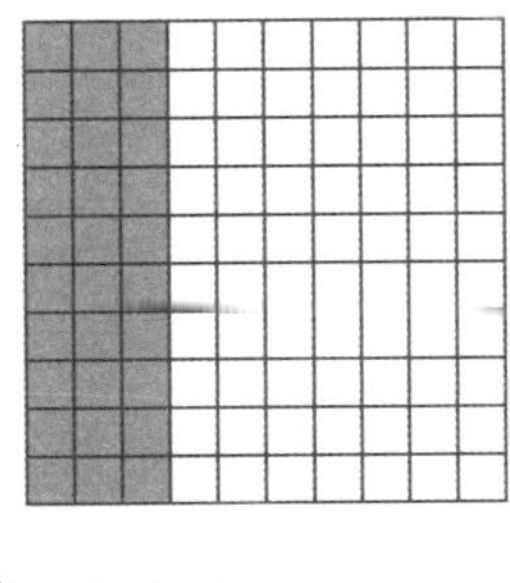

0.3 ◯ 0.30

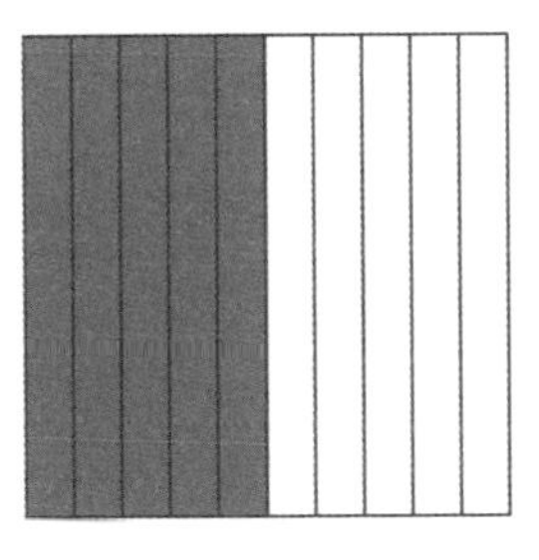 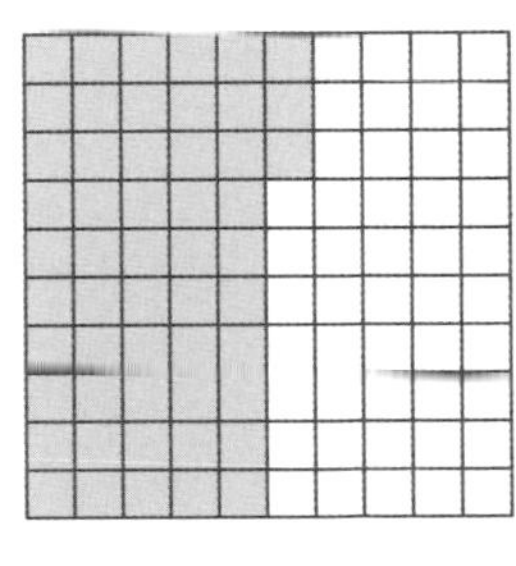

0.5 ◯ 0.53

88 Ordering decimals

Compare each pair of decimals. Fill in each circle with >, <, or =.

0.6 ◯ 0.68

0.87 ◯ 0.78

0.51 ◯ 0.59

0.09 ◯ 0.1

0.12 ◯ 0.2

0.20 ◯ 0.2

Put the decimals in order from least to greatest.

2.4 0.24 0.4   0.24 ___ 0.4 ___ 2.4 ___

1.8 0.18 8.1   ______ ______ ______

0.81 0.18 0.1   ______ ______ ______

0.77 0.7 0.07   ______ ______ ______

IXL.com
skill ID
LVX

Answer each question.

A bottle of Crazy Spice Hot Sauce holds 3.4 ounces. A bottle of Piping Pepper Hot Sauce holds 3.6 ounces. Which bottle has more hot sauce? ____________________

A blue paper clip is 4.8 centimeters long. A silver paper clip is 4.55 centimeters long. Which paper clip is longer? ____________________

A silver phone is 6.81 millimeters thick. A gold phone has a thickness of 6.18 millimeters. Which phone is thicker? ____________________

Peter has a mechanical pencil that uses 0.7 millimeter lead. Vinnie gave him 0.9 millimeter lead. Is the lead too small or too big for Peter's pencil? ____________________

Adding decimals

Let's Learn!

When you add decimals, first line up the decimal points. Then, add! Remember to bring down the decimal point into the answer.

$$\begin{array}{r} 1.53 \\ +0.24 \\ \hline 1.77 \end{array}$$

Add.

$$\begin{array}{r} \scriptstyle 1 \\ 0.15 \\ +0.37 \\ \hline 0.52 \end{array}$$

$$\begin{array}{r} 0.79 \\ +0.01 \\ \hline \end{array}$$

$$\begin{array}{r} 0.23 \\ +0.34 \\ \hline \end{array}$$

$$\begin{array}{r} 0.34 \\ +0.63 \\ \hline \end{array}$$

$$\begin{array}{r} 1.56 \\ +0.54 \\ \hline \end{array}$$

$$\begin{array}{r} 1.53 \\ +0.77 \\ \hline \end{array}$$

$$\begin{array}{r} 1.97 \\ +4.82 \\ \hline \end{array}$$

$$\begin{array}{r} 8.83 \\ +9.59 \\ \hline \end{array}$$

IXL.com
skill ID
ZEU

Let's Learn!

When you add decimals, you start by lining up the decimal points. If one of the decimals is shorter than the other, you can put a 0 at the end to line everything up. The decimal 5.2 is the same as 5.20.

$$5.2 + 3.14 \longrightarrow \begin{array}{r} 5.20 \\ +\,3.14 \\ \hline 8.34 \end{array}$$

Add.

0.5 + 0.24 = 0.74

$$\begin{array}{r} 0.50 \\ +\,0.24 \\ \hline 0.74 \end{array}$$

0.3 + 0.48 = ____________

4.6 + 0.21 = ____________

2.35 + 0.7 = ____________

1.72 + 0.3 = ____________

1.38 + 0.9 = ____________

0.99 + 0.1 = ____________

0.7 + 4.57 = ____________

Subtracting decimals

Let's Learn!

To subtract decimal numbers, first line up the decimal point. Then, subtract!

$$\begin{array}{r} 0.78 \\ -\,0.37 \\ \hline 0.41 \end{array}$$

Subtract.

$$\begin{array}{r} 0.45 \\ -\,0.12 \\ \hline 0.33 \end{array}$$

$$\begin{array}{r} 0.28 \\ -\,0.04 \\ \hline \end{array}$$

$$\begin{array}{r} 0.29 \\ -\,0.25 \\ \hline \end{array}$$

$$\begin{array}{r} 0.64 \\ -\,0.51 \\ \hline \end{array}$$

$$\begin{array}{r} 2.68 \\ -\,0.35 \\ \hline \end{array}$$

$$\begin{array}{r} 1.68 \\ -\,0.49 \\ \hline \end{array}$$

$$\begin{array}{r} 2.34 \\ -\,1.89 \\ \hline \end{array}$$

$$\begin{array}{r} 5.63 \\ -\,2.35 \\ \hline \end{array}$$

IXL.com skill ID **YDK**

Let's Learn!

When you subtract decimals, you start by lining up the decimal points. If one of the decimals is shorter than the other, you can put a 0 at the end to line everything up. Remember, 0.2 is the same as 0.20.

$$0.46 - 0.2 \longrightarrow \begin{array}{r} 0.46 \\ -\,0.20 \\ \hline 0.26 \end{array}$$

Subtract.

0.78 − 0.4 = 0.38

$$\begin{array}{r} 0.78 \\ -\,0.40 \\ \hline 0.38 \end{array}$$

0.31 − 0.2 = ________

1.65 − 0.4 = ________

3.59 − 0.7 = ________

2.6 − 0.31 = ________

4.18 − 0.6 = ________

3.57 − 1.7 = ________

1.97 − 1.89 = ________

Adding and subtracting decimals

Answer each question.

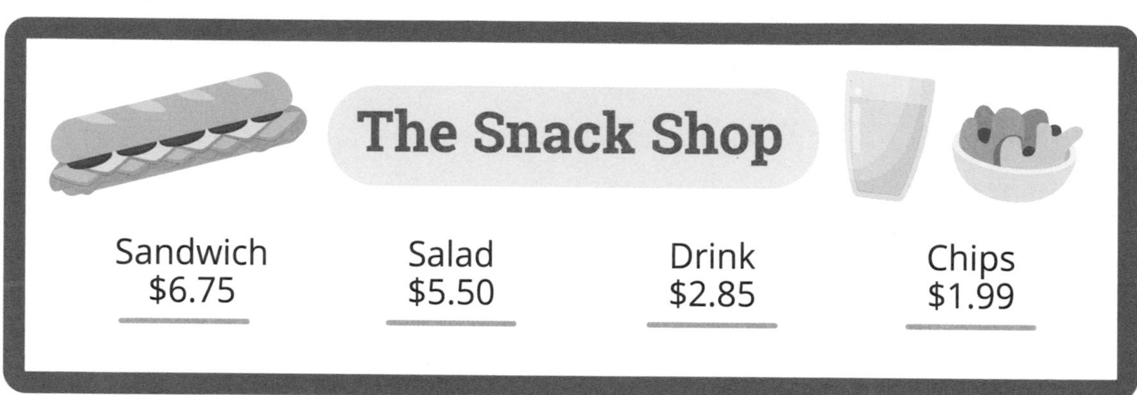

The Snack Shop
Sandwich
$6.75
Salad
$5.50
Drink
$2.85
Chips
$1.99

Carrie orders a sandwich and a drink from the Snack Shop. How much does her meal cost? ________________

Sarah orders a salad and a bag of chips. How much does her meal cost? ________________

Carrie and Sarah decide to pay together. How much do they owe altogether? ________________

Sarah has a coupon for $0.90 off. How much will the bill be after her coupon is applied? ________________

IXL.com skill ID 6HP

Finally, they pay. They hand the cashier $20.00. How much change will they get? ________________

Add or subtract.

0.45 + 0.21 = ________

0.95 − 0.6 = ________

1.98 − 0.09 = ________

1.96 − 0.8 = ________

1.7 + 0.44 = ________

1.23 + 0.9 = ________

4.88 − 2.98 = ________

1.7 − 0.84 = ________

Adding and subtracting fractions

Time to review! Add.

$\frac{2}{5} + \frac{1}{5} =$ ______

$2 + \frac{3}{4} =$ ______

$\frac{5}{12} + \frac{6}{12} =$ ______

$1\frac{2}{7} + \frac{4}{7} =$ ______

$2\frac{1}{6} + \frac{3}{6} =$ ______

$\frac{4}{9} + \frac{5}{9} =$ ______

$2\frac{4}{10} + \frac{8}{10} =$ ______

$1\frac{4}{5} + 2\frac{3}{5} =$ ______

Subtract.

$\frac{6}{8} - \frac{3}{8} =$ ______

$\frac{4}{5} - \frac{1}{5} =$ ______

$\frac{10}{11} - \frac{3}{11} =$ ______

$\frac{11}{12} - \frac{9}{12} =$ ______

$3\frac{5}{7} - \frac{3}{7} =$ ______

$5\frac{3}{4} - 1\frac{1}{4} =$ ______

$3\frac{1}{3} - 1\frac{1}{3} =$ ______

IXL.com
skill ID
9AS

Write the missing numbers.

$\frac{2}{5} + \frac{\square}{5} = \frac{4}{5}$ $\frac{\square}{8} - \frac{2}{8} = \frac{5}{8}$

$\frac{1}{7} + \frac{\square}{7} = \frac{4}{7}$ $\frac{5}{9} + \frac{\square}{9} = \frac{12}{9}$

$2\frac{1}{8} - \frac{\square}{8} = 1\frac{6}{8}$ $1\frac{\square}{9} + \frac{2}{9} = 1\frac{7}{9}$

$3\frac{\square}{12} - 1\frac{6}{12} = 2\frac{1}{12}$ $1\frac{2}{4} + 1\frac{\square}{4} = 3\frac{1}{4}$

Write the missing fractions or mixed numbers.

$\_\_\_\_ - \frac{1}{5} = \frac{3}{5}$ $\frac{5}{8} - \_\_\_\_ = \frac{3}{8}$

$1\frac{4}{5} + \_\_\_\_ = 2$ $1\frac{4}{9} - \_\_\_\_ = \frac{2}{9}$

$\_\_\_\_ + 1\frac{2}{8} = 2\frac{7}{8}$ $\frac{5}{10} + \_\_\_\_ = 1\frac{9}{10}$

$6\frac{8}{9} - \_\_\_\_ = 4\frac{3}{9}$ $1\frac{1}{10} + \_\_\_\_ = 1\frac{3}{10}$

Multiplying fractions

Fill in the blanks. Multiply the two inner numbers to get the outer number.

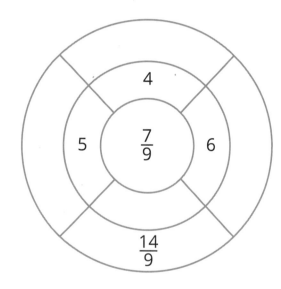

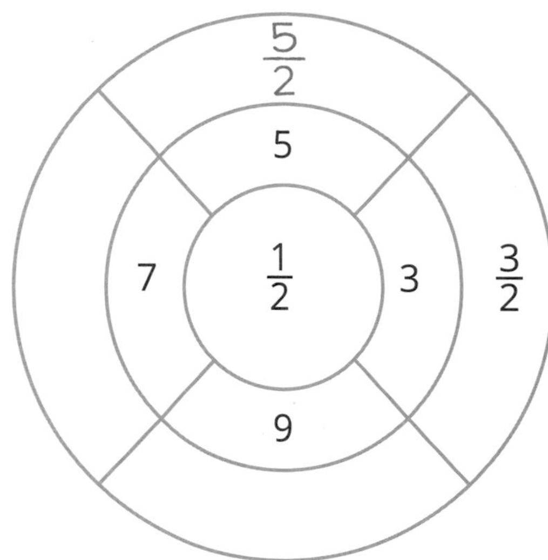

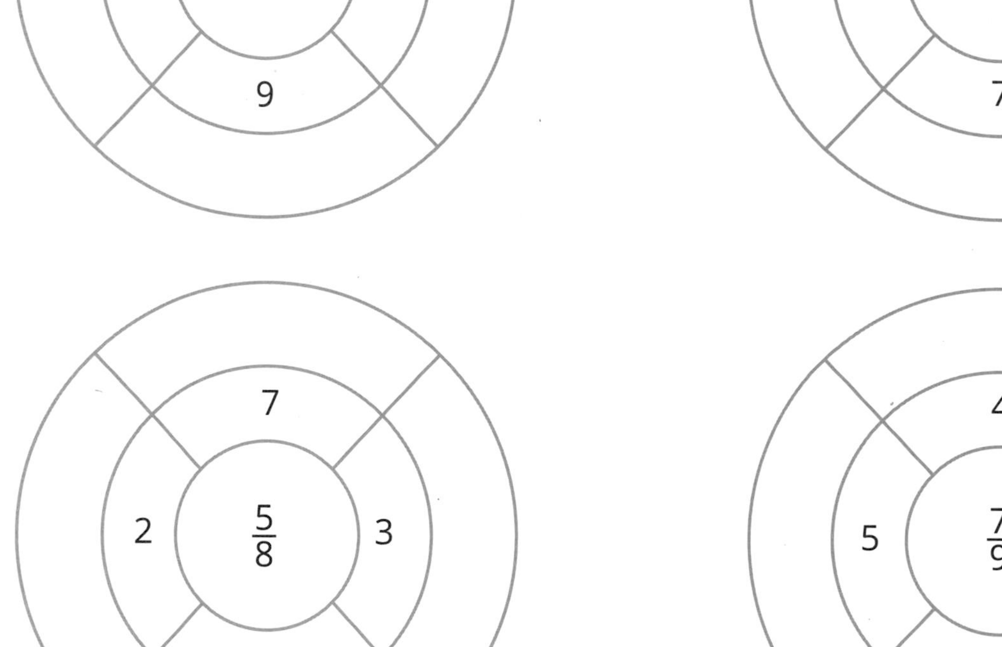

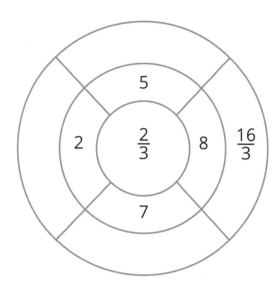

Write each fraction as a decimal.

$\frac{37}{100}$ = ________ $\frac{3}{10}$ = ________ $\frac{7}{100}$ = ________

$\frac{4}{5}$ = ________ $\frac{1}{4}$ = ________ $\frac{16}{50}$ = ________

$\frac{19}{25}$ = ________ $\frac{29}{50}$ = ________ $\frac{17}{20}$ = ________

Write each decimal as a fraction.

0.49 = ________ 0.5 = ________ 0.56 = ________

0.09 = ________ 0.2 = ________ 0.28 = ________

0.18 = ________ 0.05 = ________ 0.88 = ________

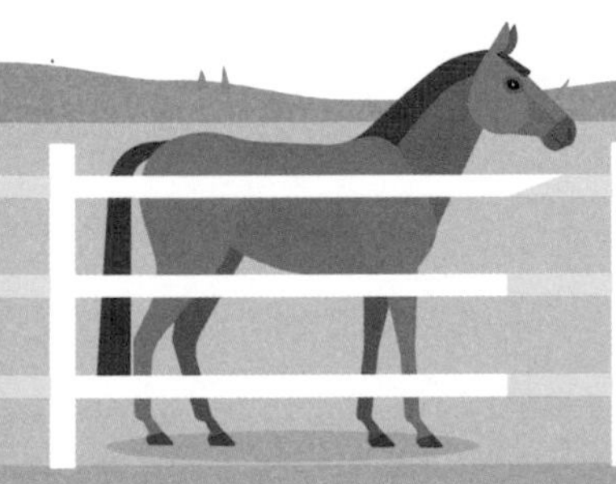

IXL.com skill ID **DBF**

Mixed operations

Add, subtract, or multiply.

$\frac{9}{10} - \frac{3}{10} =$ ______

$\frac{4}{8} + \frac{2}{8} =$ ______

$5 \times \frac{6}{7} =$ ______

$0.9 - 0.4 =$ ______

$0.25 + 0.11 =$ ______

$\frac{29}{5} - \frac{17}{5} =$ ______

$1\frac{2}{3} + \frac{2}{3} =$ ______

$0.65 - 0.2 =$ ______

$2\frac{5}{12} - 1\frac{3}{12} =$ ______

$3\frac{3}{5} + 2\frac{3}{5} =$ ______

$1.18 - 0.48 =$ ______

$0.34 + 0.89 =$ ______

Add, subtract, or multiply.

$8 \times \frac{6}{9} =$ ________

$0.38 - 0.29 =$ ________

$0.77 + 0.14 =$ ________

$6\frac{1}{4} - 1\frac{1}{4} =$ ________

$6\frac{1}{5} + 2\frac{2}{5} =$ ________

$12 \times \frac{2}{9} =$ ________

$1.5 + 0.31 =$ ________

$2\frac{1}{7} - 1\frac{4}{7} =$ ________

$2.25 - 0.71 =$ ________

$6 \times \frac{5}{6} =$ ________

$0.8 - 0.19 =$ ________

$0.67 + 0.4 =$ ________

$0.42 + 1.09 =$ ________

$4\frac{1}{9} - 2\frac{2}{9} =$ ________

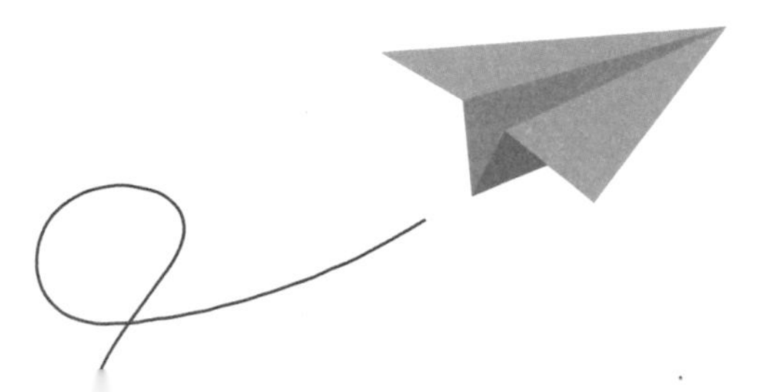

Answer each question.

Nina's Labrador puppy, Lyla, weighed 1.1 pounds when she was born. At her three-month checkup, Lyla had gained 23.8 pounds. Lyla gained 24.5 more pounds by the time she was six months old. How much did Lyla weigh when she was six months old? ____________

Connor had a piece of wood that was $1\frac{3}{4}$ feet long. He then cut off three $\frac{1}{2}$-foot pieces. How much of the original wood was left? ____________

Derek paid for a movie ticket and a bag of popcorn with a $20 bill. If the movie ticket cost $7.75 and the popcorn cost $4.99, how much change did Derek receive? ____________

Bella's class voted on what kind of fundraiser to do this year. After looking at the results, Bella noticed that $\frac{3}{8}$ of the class wanted to host an outdoor movie, $\frac{4}{8}$ of the class wanted to have a car wash, and $\frac{1}{8}$ of the class wanted to have a talent show in the auditorium. If there are 24 students in Bella's class, how many students wanted to have a movie or car wash? ____________

IXL.com
skill ID
YLH

Answer each question.

Josie wants to make a fruit salad. She buys 2.3 pounds of apples, 1.78 pounds of oranges, and 0.95 pounds of blueberries. How many pounds of fruit does she buy in all? ______________

Each month, Maggie uses $\frac{3}{4}$ of a jar of peanut butter. How many jars of peanut butter would Maggie need for 1 year? ______________

At a yard sale, Holden buys a scooter for $12.50 and a poster for $2.75. If Holden pays with a $20 bill, how much change will he get? ______________

Greg bought three $\frac{1}{2}$-gallon jugs of milk. He used $\frac{1}{16}$ of a gallon of milk for cereal and $\frac{2}{16}$ of a gallon for a glass of chocolate milk. How much milk does Greg have left over? ______________

IXL.com skill ID YKM

Answer key

Fractions can be written in lots of equivalent ways! This answer key includes both the answer your child is most likely to write down and its simplest form. Keep in mind that other answers may also be correct.

PAGE 2

$\frac{1}{2}$ $\frac{2}{3}$ $\frac{3}{4}$

$\frac{2}{4}$ or $\frac{1}{2}$ $\frac{7}{8}$ $\frac{4}{6}$ or $\frac{2}{3}$

PAGE 3

$\frac{1}{3}$ $\frac{3}{4}$ $\frac{5}{8}$ $\frac{2}{6}$ or $\frac{1}{3}$

PAGE 4

$\frac{2}{5}$ $\frac{2}{4}$ or $\frac{1}{2}$ $\frac{1}{7}$ $\frac{6}{8}$ or $\frac{3}{4}$

PAGE 5

$\frac{6}{9}$ or $\frac{2}{3}$ $\frac{2}{8}$ or $\frac{1}{4}$ $\frac{6}{12}$ or $\frac{1}{2}$

$\frac{2}{4}$ or $\frac{1}{2}$ $\frac{2}{6}$ or $\frac{1}{3}$ $\frac{10}{12}$ or $\frac{5}{6}$

$\frac{3}{7}$ $\frac{7}{10}$

PAGE 6

Placement of shading may vary.

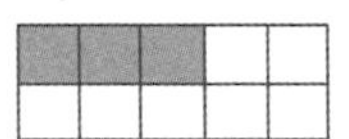
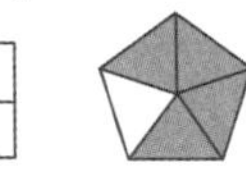

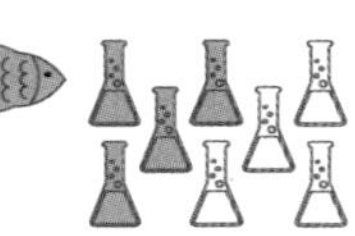

Drawings may vary.

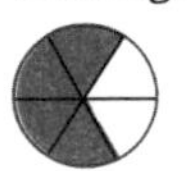
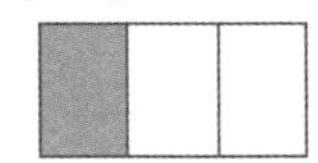
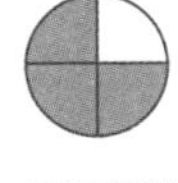
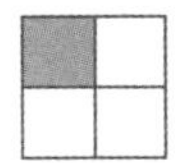
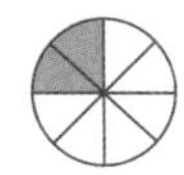
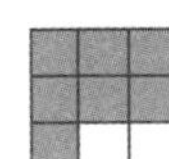

PAGE 7

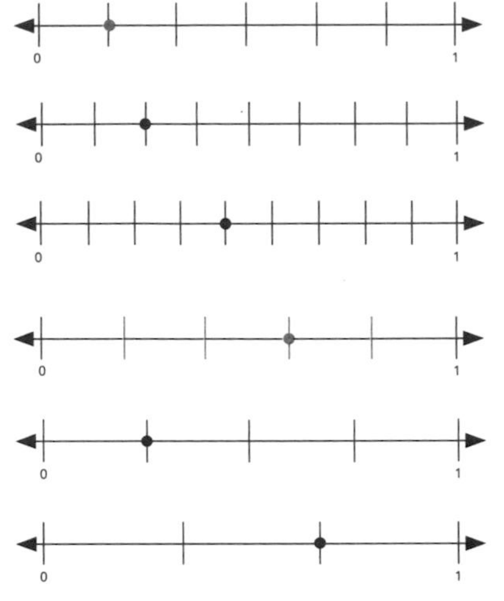

PAGE 8

$\frac{4}{12}$ $\frac{7}{8}$ $\frac{4}{9}$

$\frac{5}{6}$ $\frac{5}{8}$

PAGE 9

Answers may vary. Some possible answers are shown below.

$\frac{3}{4}$ $\frac{3}{6}$

$\frac{2}{5}$ $\frac{4}{5}$

$\frac{1}{6}$ $\frac{5}{8}$

PAGE 10

$\frac{1}{2} = \frac{2}{4}$ $\frac{2}{3} = \frac{4}{6}$

$\frac{3}{5} = \frac{6}{10}$ $\frac{1}{3} = \frac{3}{9}$

PAGE 11

$\frac{1}{5} = \frac{2}{10}$ $\frac{2}{6} = \frac{1}{3}$

$\frac{4}{8} = \frac{2}{4}$ $\frac{2}{6} = \frac{4}{12}$

$\frac{3}{4} = \frac{6}{8}$ $\frac{4}{16} = \frac{2}{8}$

PAGE 12

$\frac{1}{4} = \frac{2}{8}$ $\frac{1}{2} = \frac{3}{6}$ $\frac{5}{6} = \frac{10}{12}$

PAGE 13

$\frac{4}{5} = \frac{8}{10}$ $\frac{2}{6} = \frac{4}{12}$ $\frac{1}{4} = \frac{3}{12}$

$\frac{2}{3} = \frac{6}{9}$ $\frac{3}{8} = \frac{6}{16}$ $\frac{2}{5} = \frac{6}{15}$

PAGE 14

5: 1, 5
10: 1, 2, 5, 10 $\frac{5}{10} = \frac{1}{2}$

7: 1, 7
21: 1, 3, 7, 21 $\frac{7}{21} = \frac{1}{3}$

Equivalent fractions may vary.
18: 1, 2, 3, 6, 9, 18
24: 1, 2, 3, 4, 6, 8, 12, 24 $\frac{18}{24} = \frac{3}{4}$

PAGE 15

$\frac{1}{3} = \frac{3}{9}$ $\frac{5}{6} = \frac{10}{12}$

$\frac{6}{8} = \frac{3}{4}$ $\frac{3}{4} = \frac{12}{16}$

$\frac{12}{18} = \frac{2}{3}$ $\frac{9}{24} = \frac{3}{8}$

PAGE 16

Answers may vary. Some possible answers are shown below.

$\frac{3}{5} = \frac{12}{20}$ $\frac{2}{4} = \frac{1}{2}$

$\frac{2}{3} = \frac{4}{6}$ $\frac{5}{20} = \frac{1}{4}$

$\frac{6}{16} = \frac{3}{8}$ $\frac{4}{18} = \frac{2}{9}$

$\frac{2}{10} = \frac{1}{5}$ $\frac{7}{8} = \frac{14}{16}$

$\frac{12}{16} = \frac{3}{4}$ $\frac{14}{21} = \frac{2}{3}$

Here are other possible equivalent fractions for each problem.

$\frac{3}{5} = \frac{6}{10} = \frac{9}{15}$ $\frac{2}{4} = \frac{4}{8} = \frac{8}{16}$

$\frac{2}{3} = \frac{6}{9} = \frac{8}{12}$ $\frac{5}{20} = \frac{10}{40} = \frac{20}{80}$

$\frac{6}{16} = \frac{12}{32} = \frac{24}{64}$ $\frac{4}{18} = \frac{8}{36} = \frac{16}{72}$

$\frac{2}{10} = \frac{4}{20} = \frac{8}{40}$ $\frac{7}{8} = \frac{21}{24} = \frac{28}{32}$

$\frac{12}{16} = \frac{6}{8} = \frac{24}{32}$ $\frac{14}{21} = \frac{28}{42} = \frac{42}{63}$

PAGE 17

$\frac{3}{9}$	$\frac{5}{6}$
$\frac{10}{15}$	$\frac{4}{9}$
$\frac{8}{18}$	$\frac{4}{22}$
$\frac{12}{21}$	$\frac{3}{6}$
$\frac{2}{11}$	$\frac{4}{7}$
$\frac{10}{12}$	$\frac{2}{3}$
$\frac{1}{2}$	$\frac{1}{3}$

PAGE 18

no, $\frac{2}{3}$ yes

yes no, $\frac{1}{2}$

no, $\frac{2}{5}$ yes

no, $\frac{3}{5}$ no, $\frac{3}{4}$

PAGE 19

$\frac{2}{3} > \frac{1}{3}$ $\frac{3}{5} < \frac{4}{5}$

$\frac{1}{6} < \frac{3}{6}$ $\frac{2}{5} = \frac{2}{5}$

$\frac{8}{10} > \frac{7}{10}$ $\frac{5}{9} > \frac{3}{9}$

$\frac{8}{12} > \frac{6}{12}$ $\frac{7}{8} > \frac{5}{8}$

PAGE 20

$\frac{1}{3} > \frac{1}{6}$ $\frac{1}{4} < \frac{1}{3}$

$\frac{1}{2} > \frac{1}{4}$ $\frac{1}{6} > \frac{1}{9}$

$\frac{1}{6} > \frac{1}{7}$ $\frac{1}{2} > \frac{1}{3}$ $\frac{1}{8} < \frac{1}{4}$ $\frac{1}{4} > \frac{1}{6}$

PAGE 21

$\frac{3}{4} > \frac{3}{6}$ $\frac{5}{8} < \frac{5}{6}$ $\frac{2}{6} < \frac{2}{3}$

$\frac{6}{9} > \frac{6}{10}$ $\frac{3}{8} > \frac{3}{12}$ $\frac{2}{10} < \frac{2}{8}$

$\frac{3}{4} > \frac{1}{6}$ $\frac{2}{10} < \frac{3}{8}$ $\frac{4}{6} > \frac{3}{7}$

PAGE 22

$\frac{4}{6} > \frac{1}{2}$ $\frac{4}{10} < \frac{1}{2}$

PAGE 23

($\frac{3}{4}$) $\frac{1}{6}$ ($\frac{7}{8}$)

($\frac{5}{6}$) $\frac{2}{9}$ $\frac{1}{4}$

($\frac{2}{3}$) $\frac{3}{8}$ ($\frac{6}{7}$)

$\frac{1}{3}$ ($\frac{6}{10}$) $\frac{4}{9}$

$\frac{5}{12}$ ($\frac{8}{10}$) $\frac{3}{11}$

PAGE 24

$\frac{4}{10} < \frac{5}{8}$ $\frac{7}{8} > \frac{2}{6}$ $\frac{9}{10} > \frac{1}{3}$

$\frac{4}{6} > \frac{3}{8}$ $\frac{2}{4} = \frac{3}{6}$ $\frac{4}{12} < \frac{5}{8}$

$\frac{2}{5} < \frac{6}{7}$ $\frac{4}{5} > \frac{3}{8}$ $\frac{5}{10} = \frac{6}{12}$

$\frac{4}{10} < \frac{5}{6}$ $\frac{6}{10} > \frac{5}{12}$ $\frac{7}{9} > \frac{2}{11}$

PAGE 25

$\frac{2}{4} < \frac{5}{8}$ $\frac{3}{5} > \frac{2}{10}$

$\frac{1}{3} = \frac{2}{6}$ $\frac{6}{12} < \frac{3}{4}$

$\frac{7}{8} > \frac{3}{4}$ $\frac{6}{10} > \frac{1}{2}$

$\frac{5}{12} > \frac{1}{3}$

PAGE 26

15 $\frac{5}{15} < \frac{6}{15}$ 10 $\frac{4}{10} = \frac{4}{10}$

8 $\frac{6}{8} < \frac{7}{8}$ 18 $\frac{10}{18} < \frac{12}{18}$

PAGE 27

$\frac{2}{5} > \frac{3}{10}$ $\frac{1}{2} > \frac{2}{6}$ $\frac{1}{3} = \frac{2}{6}$

$\frac{5}{8} < \frac{3}{4}$ $\frac{5}{6} > \frac{7}{12}$ $\frac{2}{9} < \frac{1}{3}$

$\frac{7}{12} < \frac{2}{3}$ $\frac{5}{8} > \frac{2}{4}$ $\frac{7}{10} > \frac{1}{2}$

$\frac{6}{9} = \frac{2}{3}$ $\frac{1}{2} > \frac{1}{3}$ $\frac{2}{5} < \frac{1}{2}$

$\frac{3}{4} > \frac{2}{3}$ $\frac{3}{4} > \frac{4}{6}$ $\frac{4}{6} > \frac{5}{8}$

PAGE 28

$\frac{1}{2}$ $\frac{2}{3}$ $\frac{5}{6}$

$\frac{1}{6}$ $\frac{1}{2}$ $\frac{6}{7}$

$\frac{3}{8}$ $\frac{1}{2}$ $\frac{3}{4}$

$\frac{1}{3}$ $\frac{4}{6}$ $\frac{7}{9}$

$\frac{5}{12}$ $\frac{2}{3}$ $\frac{3}{4}$

$\frac{1}{3}$ $\frac{2}{5}$ $\frac{2}{4}$

$\frac{1}{4}$ $\frac{2}{6}$ $\frac{2}{3}$

PAGE 29

Aaron
Rex
Penny
the preschool

PAGE 30

Placement of shading may vary.

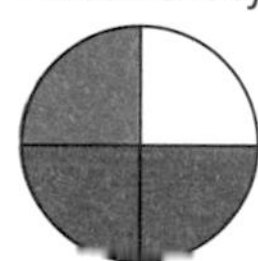

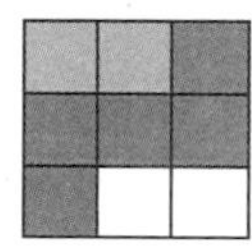

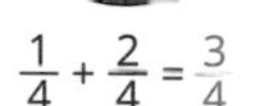

$\frac{1}{4} + \frac{2}{4} = \frac{3}{4}$

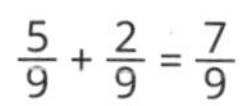

$\frac{5}{9} + \frac{2}{9} = \frac{7}{9}$

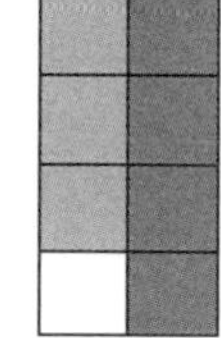

$\frac{3}{8} + \frac{4}{8} = \frac{7}{8}$

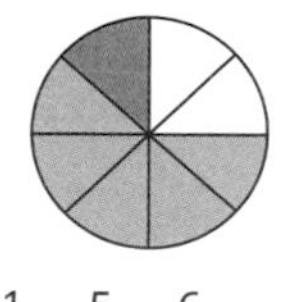

$\frac{1}{8} + \frac{5}{8} = \frac{6}{8}$ or $\frac{3}{4}$

When you add fractions with the same denominator, add the numerators. The denominator will stay the same.

Answer key

PAGE 31

$\frac{1}{4}+\frac{1}{4}=\frac{2}{4}$

$\frac{1}{9}+\frac{1}{9}+\frac{1}{9}=\frac{3}{9}$

$\frac{1}{8}+\frac{1}{8}+\frac{1}{8}+\frac{1}{8}+\frac{1}{8}=\frac{5}{8}$

$\frac{5}{10}=\frac{1}{10}+\frac{1}{10}+\frac{1}{10}+\frac{1}{10}+\frac{1}{10}$

$\frac{6}{7}=\frac{1}{7}+\frac{1}{7}+\frac{1}{7}+\frac{1}{7}+\frac{1}{7}+\frac{1}{7}$

PAGE 32

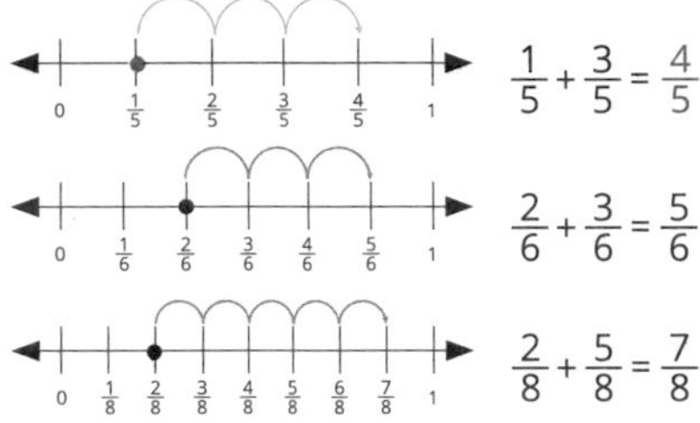

$\frac{1}{5}+\frac{3}{5}=\frac{4}{5}$

$\frac{2}{6}+\frac{3}{6}=\frac{5}{6}$

$\frac{2}{8}+\frac{5}{8}=\frac{7}{8}$

$\frac{4}{10}+\frac{3}{10}=\frac{7}{10}$

PAGE 33

$\frac{1}{8}+\frac{2}{8}=\frac{3}{8}$ $\quad$ $\frac{1}{3}+\frac{1}{3}=\frac{2}{3}$

$\frac{2}{5}+\frac{2}{5}=\frac{4}{5}$ $\quad$ $\frac{3}{6}+\frac{2}{6}=\frac{5}{6}$

$\frac{2}{7}+\frac{1}{7}=\frac{3}{7}$ $\quad$ $\frac{5}{9}+\frac{3}{9}=\frac{8}{9}$

$\frac{1}{5}+\frac{3}{5}=\frac{4}{5}$ $\quad$ $\frac{6}{10}+\frac{2}{10}=\frac{8}{10}$ or $\frac{4}{5}$

$\frac{1}{4}+\frac{1}{4}=\frac{2}{4}$ $\quad$ $\frac{1}{6}+\frac{4}{6}=\frac{5}{6}$

$\frac{1}{8}+\frac{5}{8}=\frac{6}{8}$ $\quad$ $\frac{2}{7}+\frac{2}{7}=\frac{4}{7}$

PAGE 34

$\frac{1}{4}+\frac{2}{4}=\frac{3}{4}$

$\frac{5}{9}+\frac{2}{9}=\frac{7}{9}$

$\frac{4}{12}+\frac{5}{12}=\frac{9}{12}$ or $\frac{3}{4}$

$\frac{7}{10}+\frac{2}{10}=\frac{9}{10}$

PAGE 35

$\frac{3}{8}+\frac{1}{8}+\frac{1}{8}=\frac{5}{8}$

$\frac{2}{10}+\frac{3}{10}+\frac{4}{10}=\frac{9}{10}$

$\frac{1}{6}+\frac{2}{6}+\frac{2}{6}=\frac{5}{6}$

$\frac{1}{9}+\frac{3}{9}+\frac{4}{9}=\frac{8}{9}$

$\frac{3}{12}+\frac{3}{12}+\frac{3}{12}=\frac{9}{12}$ or $\frac{3}{4}$

$\frac{5}{10}+\frac{1}{10}+\frac{2}{10}=\frac{8}{10}$ or $\frac{4}{5}$

$\frac{1}{6}+\frac{2}{6}+\frac{1}{6}=\frac{4}{6}$ or $\frac{2}{3}$

$\frac{1}{8}+\frac{2}{8}+\frac{4}{8}=\frac{7}{8}$

$\frac{3}{7}+\frac{1}{7}+\frac{2}{7}=\frac{6}{7}$

$\frac{2}{11}+\frac{4}{11}+\frac{2}{11}=\frac{8}{11}$

PAGE 36

$\frac{1}{6}+\frac{1}{6}=\frac{2}{6}=\frac{1}{3}$ $\quad$ $\frac{1}{5}+\frac{3}{5}=\frac{4}{5}$

$\frac{1}{8}+\frac{3}{8}=\frac{4}{8}=\frac{1}{2}$ $\quad$ $\frac{1}{4}+\frac{1}{4}=\frac{2}{4}=\frac{1}{2}$

$\frac{1}{3}+\frac{1}{3}=\frac{2}{3}$ $\quad$ $\frac{1}{6}+\frac{1}{6}=\frac{2}{6}=\frac{1}{3}$

$\frac{3}{10}+\frac{1}{10}=\frac{4}{10}=\frac{2}{5}$ $\quad$ $\frac{4}{7}+\frac{2}{7}=\frac{6}{7}$

$\frac{5}{12}+\frac{1}{12}=\frac{6}{12}=\frac{1}{2}$ $\quad$ $\frac{5}{8}+\frac{1}{8}=\frac{6}{8}=\frac{3}{4}$

PAGE 37

A

$\frac{1}{3}+\frac{1}{3}$	$\frac{1}{8}+\frac{2}{8}$	$\frac{2}{9}+\frac{5}{9}$
$\frac{2}{9}+\frac{4}{9}$	$\frac{2}{3}+\frac{1}{3}$	$\frac{4}{12}+\frac{4}{12}$
$\frac{3}{12}+\frac{5}{12}$	$\frac{1}{6}+\frac{4}{6}$	$\frac{1}{9}+\frac{2}{9}$
$\frac{2}{6}+\frac{2}{6}$	$\frac{1}{6}+\frac{1}{6}$	$\frac{2}{12}+\frac{2}{12}$

B

PAGE 38

Placement of shading may vary.

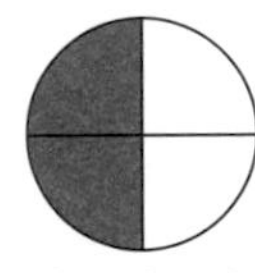

$\frac{3}{4}-\frac{1}{4}=\frac{2}{4}$

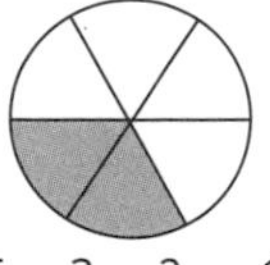

$\frac{5}{6}-\frac{3}{6}=\frac{2}{6}$ or $\frac{1}{3}$

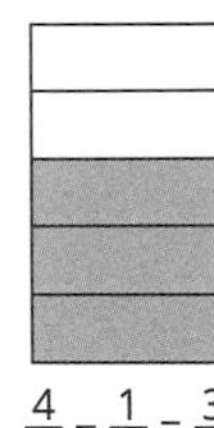

$\frac{4}{5}-\frac{1}{5}=\frac{3}{5}$

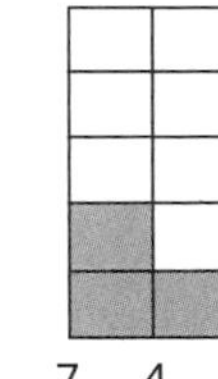

$\frac{7}{10}-\frac{4}{10}=\frac{3}{10}$

PAGE 39

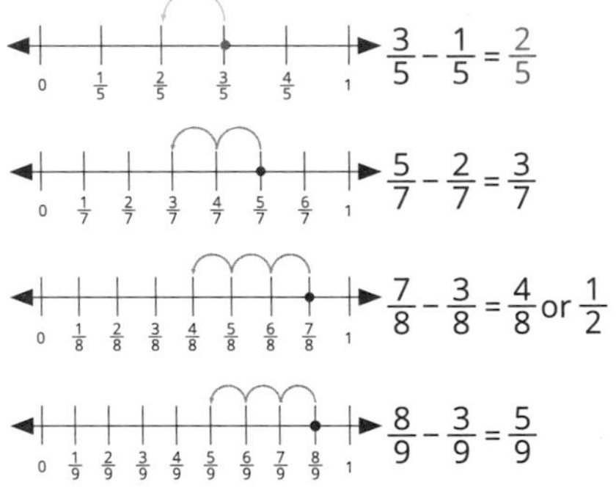

$\frac{3}{5}-\frac{1}{5}=\frac{2}{5}$

$\frac{5}{7}-\frac{2}{7}=\frac{3}{7}$

$\frac{7}{8}-\frac{3}{8}=\frac{4}{8}$ or $\frac{1}{2}$

$\frac{8}{9}-\frac{3}{9}=\frac{5}{9}$

PAGE 40

$\frac{4}{5}-\frac{1}{5}=\frac{3}{5}$ $\quad$ $\frac{3}{4}-\frac{2}{4}=\frac{1}{4}$

$\frac{2}{3}-\frac{1}{3}=\frac{1}{3}$ $\quad$ $\frac{6}{9}-\frac{2}{9}=\frac{4}{9}$

$\frac{4}{6}-\frac{3}{6}=\frac{1}{6}$ $\quad$ $\frac{8}{9}-\frac{6}{9}=\frac{2}{9}$

$\frac{9}{10}-\frac{3}{10}=\frac{6}{10}$ or $\frac{3}{5}$ $\quad$ $\frac{10}{12}-\frac{7}{12}=\frac{3}{12}$ or $\frac{1}{4}$

PAGE 41

$\frac{3}{5}-\frac{1}{5}=\frac{2}{5}$ $\quad$ $\frac{6}{12}-\frac{4}{12}=\frac{2}{12}$ $\quad$ $\frac{5}{8}-\frac{4}{8}=\frac{1}{8}$

$\frac{11}{12}-\frac{3}{12}=\frac{8}{12}$ $\quad$ $\frac{6}{7}-\frac{1}{7}=\frac{5}{7}$ $\quad$ $\frac{8}{9}-\frac{5}{9}=\frac{3}{9}$

$\frac{3}{4}-\frac{1}{4}=\frac{2}{4}$ $\quad$ $\frac{9}{10}-\frac{6}{10}=\frac{3}{10}$ $\quad$ $\frac{4}{5}-\frac{2}{5}=\frac{2}{5}$

$\frac{7}{11}-\frac{6}{11}=\frac{1}{11}$ $\quad$ $\frac{5}{12}-\frac{1}{12}=\frac{4}{12}$ $\quad$ $\frac{3}{6}-\frac{1}{6}=\frac{2}{6}$

Answers may vary. Some possible answers are shown below.

$\frac{4}{5}-\frac{3}{5}=\frac{1}{5}$ $\quad$ $\frac{7}{8}-\frac{2}{8}=\frac{5}{8}$ $\quad$ $\frac{8}{10}-\frac{6}{10}=\frac{2}{10}$

PAGE 42

$\frac{11}{12} - \frac{3}{12} = \frac{8}{12}$ or $\frac{2}{3}$ of a yard

$\frac{5}{8} - \frac{3}{8} = \frac{2}{8}$ or $\frac{1}{4}$ of the walls

$\frac{6}{8} - \frac{1}{8} = \frac{5}{8}$ of the cake

$\frac{5}{7} - \frac{3}{7} = \frac{2}{7}$ of his money

$\frac{8}{10} - \frac{5}{10} = \frac{3}{10}$ of a pound

PAGE 43

$\frac{2}{9} + \frac{6}{9} = \frac{8}{9}$

$\frac{4}{5} - \frac{2}{5} = \frac{2}{5}$

$\frac{6}{10} - \frac{3}{10} = \frac{3}{10}$

$\frac{7}{8} - \frac{4}{8} = \frac{3}{8}$

$\frac{3}{10} + \frac{4}{10} = \frac{7}{10}$

$\frac{3}{4} - \frac{1}{4} = \frac{2}{4}$ or $\frac{1}{2}$

$\frac{1}{6} + \frac{3}{6} = \frac{4}{6}$ or $\frac{2}{3}$

$\frac{7}{12} + \frac{2}{12} = \frac{9}{12}$ or $\frac{3}{4}$

$\frac{5}{11} + \frac{5}{11} = \frac{10}{11}$

$\frac{5}{6} - \frac{3}{6} = \frac{2}{6}$ or $\frac{1}{3}$

PAGE 44

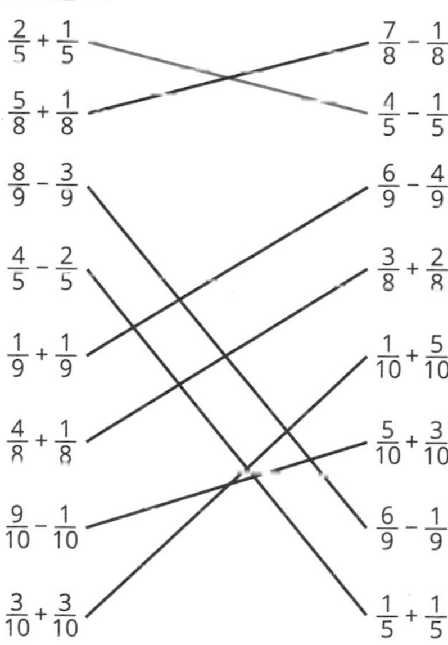

PAGE 45

$\frac{7}{8} - \frac{6}{8} = \frac{1}{8}$ of a cup

$\frac{2}{8} - \frac{1}{8} = \frac{1}{8}$ of a cup

$\frac{3}{4} - \frac{1}{4} = \frac{2}{4}$ or $\frac{1}{2}$ of a teaspoon

$\frac{4}{12} + \frac{6}{12} = \frac{10}{12}$ or $\frac{5}{6}$ of a cup

PAGE 46

$\frac{5}{20} + \frac{7}{20} = \frac{12}{20}$ or $\frac{3}{5}$

$\frac{8}{54} + \frac{6}{54} = \frac{14}{54}$ or $\frac{7}{27}$

$\frac{11}{30} + \frac{12}{30} = \frac{23}{30}$

$\frac{45}{59} - \frac{32}{50} = \frac{13}{50}$

$\frac{56}{90} + \frac{31}{90} = \frac{87}{90}$ or $\frac{29}{30}$

$\frac{10}{40} - \frac{5}{40} = \frac{5}{40}$ or $\frac{1}{8}$

$\frac{9}{25} + \frac{7}{25} = \frac{16}{25}$

$\frac{17}{19} - \frac{14}{19} = \frac{3}{19}$

$\frac{28}{35} - \frac{14}{35} = \frac{14}{35}$ or $\frac{2}{5}$

$\frac{72}{80} - \frac{59}{80} = \frac{13}{80}$

PAGE 47

Placement of shading may vary.

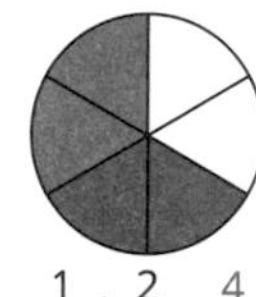

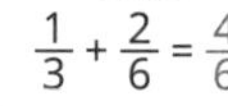

$\frac{1}{3} + \frac{2}{6} = \frac{4}{6}$

$\frac{1}{4} + \frac{3}{8} = \frac{5}{8}$

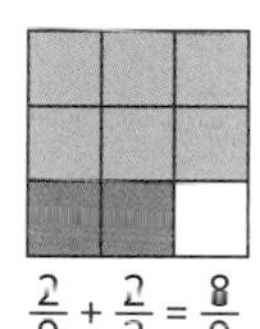

$\frac{2}{9} + \frac{2}{3} = \frac{8}{9}$

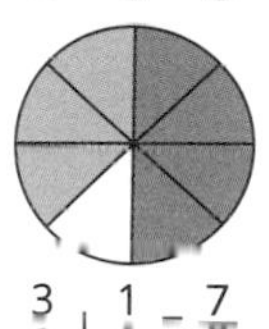

$\frac{3}{8} + \frac{1}{2} = \frac{7}{8}$

PAGE 48

$\frac{4}{12} + \frac{3}{12} = \frac{7}{12}$

$\frac{3}{21} + \frac{14}{21} = \frac{17}{21}$

$\frac{3}{12} + \frac{4}{12} = \frac{7}{12}$

$\frac{10}{15} + \frac{3}{15} = \frac{13}{15}$

$\frac{2}{10} + \frac{5}{10} = \frac{7}{10}$

$\frac{4}{12} + \frac{6}{12} = \frac{10}{12}$ or $\frac{5}{6}$

$\frac{8}{12} + \frac{3}{12} = \frac{11}{12}$

$\frac{7}{14} + \frac{6}{14} = \frac{13}{14}$

PAGE 49

$4\frac{1}{2}$ $2\frac{2}{3}$ $4\frac{6}{10}$ or $4\frac{3}{5}$ $3\frac{5}{6}$

PAGE 50

$3\frac{1}{2}$ $1\frac{2}{4}$ or $1\frac{1}{2}$ $1\frac{3}{5}$ $2\frac{5}{6}$

PAGE 51

Drawings may vary.

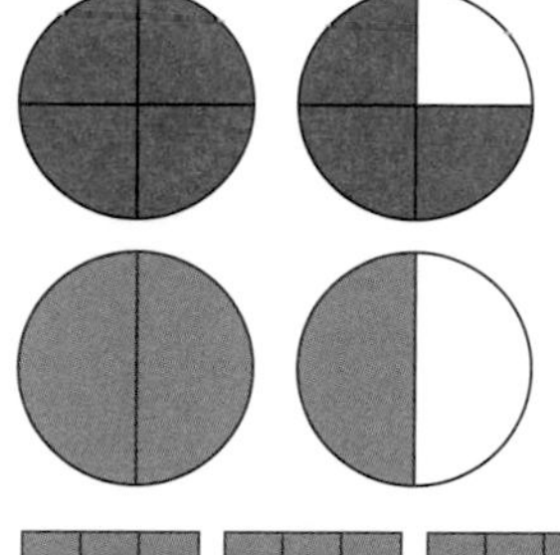

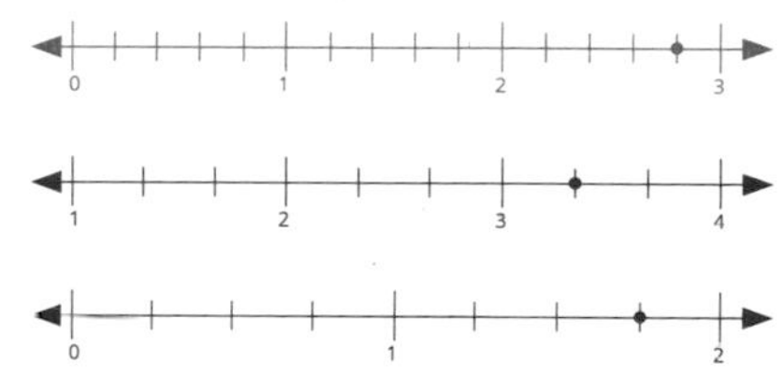

PAGE 52

$\frac{7}{2}$ $\frac{11}{4}$ $\frac{7}{3}$ $\frac{11}{8}$

PAGE 53

$\frac{7}{4} = 1\frac{3}{4}$

$\frac{7}{2} = 3\frac{1}{2}$

$\frac{15}{3} = 5$

$\frac{20}{6} = 3\frac{2}{6}$ or $3\frac{1}{3}$

PAGE 54

$\frac{14}{4} = 3\frac{2}{4}$

$\frac{41}{9} = 4\frac{5}{9}$

$\frac{31}{11} = 2\frac{9}{11}$

$\frac{10}{3} = 3\frac{1}{3}$

$\frac{23}{12} = 1\frac{11}{12}$

$\frac{40}{7} = 5\frac{5}{7}$

$4\frac{1}{2} = \frac{9}{2}$

$3\frac{4}{10} = \frac{34}{10}$ or $\frac{17}{5}$

$6\frac{4}{7} = \frac{46}{7}$

$5\frac{1}{4} = \frac{21}{4}$

$5\frac{7}{8} = \frac{47}{8}$

$7\frac{5}{11} = \frac{82}{11}$

Answer key

PAGE 55

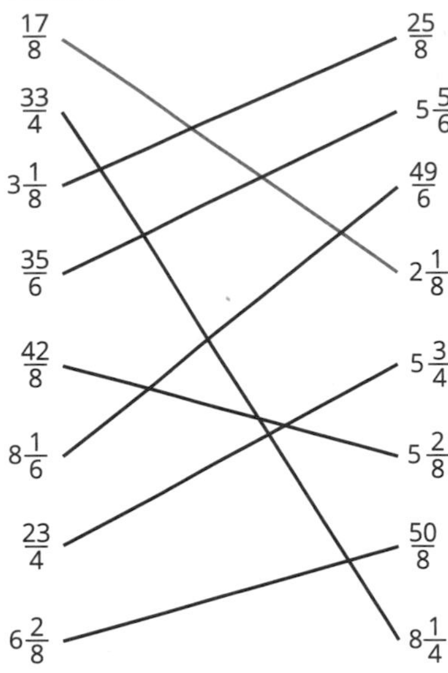

PAGE 56

9 scoops

11 cups

15 laps

PAGE 57

$2\frac{1}{4}+4\frac{2}{4}=6\frac{3}{4}$

$3\frac{1}{3}+1\frac{1}{3}=4\frac{2}{3}$

$2\frac{3}{6}+2\frac{1}{6}=4\frac{4}{6}$ or $4\frac{2}{3}$

$3\frac{3}{8}+4\frac{4}{8}=7\frac{7}{8}$

$4\frac{1}{5}+2\frac{2}{5}=6\frac{3}{5}$

$6\frac{1}{9}+3\frac{4}{9}=9\frac{5}{9}$

PAGE 58

$2\frac{3}{5}+1\frac{4}{5}=4\frac{2}{5}$

$3\frac{5}{6}+1\frac{3}{6}=5\frac{2}{6}$ or $5\frac{1}{3}$

$5\frac{7}{8}+3\frac{7}{8}=9\frac{6}{8}$ or $9\frac{3}{4}$

$4\frac{3}{6}+2\frac{4}{6}=7\frac{1}{6}$

$3\frac{4}{5}+5\frac{4}{5}=9\frac{3}{5}$

$1\frac{3}{9}+4\frac{7}{9}=6\frac{1}{9}$

PAGE 59

$1\frac{2}{7}+2\frac{3}{7}=3\frac{5}{7}$

$2\frac{3}{8}+4\frac{1}{8}=6\frac{4}{8}$ or $6\frac{1}{2}$

$1\frac{2}{4}+2\frac{1}{4}=3\frac{3}{4}$

$5\frac{3}{6}+1\frac{1}{6}=6\frac{4}{6}$ or $6\frac{2}{3}$

$6\frac{1}{5}+3\frac{3}{5}=9\frac{4}{5}$

$6\frac{2}{10}+8\frac{5}{10}=14\frac{7}{10}$

$3\frac{3}{4}+2\frac{2}{4}=6\frac{1}{4}$

$5\frac{5}{6}+2\frac{2}{6}=8\frac{1}{6}$

$7\frac{4}{8}+2\frac{4}{8}=10$

$2\frac{8}{9}+4\frac{7}{9}=7\frac{6}{9}$ or $7\frac{2}{3}$

PAGE 60

$1\frac{3}{12}+5\frac{7}{12}=6\frac{10}{12}$ or $6\frac{5}{6}$ feet

$3\frac{3}{4}+1\frac{1}{4}=5$ cups

$5\frac{3}{4}+6\frac{2}{4}=12\frac{1}{4}$ meters

$2\frac{6}{10}+3\frac{5}{10}=6\frac{1}{10}$ miles

PAGE 61

$3\frac{3}{4}-2\frac{2}{4}=1\frac{1}{4}$

$4\frac{2}{3}-2\frac{1}{3}=2\frac{1}{3}$

$3\frac{4}{5}-2\frac{1}{5}=1\frac{3}{5}$

$4\frac{5}{6}-1\frac{3}{6}=3\frac{2}{6}$ or $3\frac{1}{3}$

$5\frac{5}{8}-2\frac{4}{8}=3\frac{1}{8}$

$4\frac{5}{7}-1\frac{3}{7}=3\frac{2}{7}$

PAGE 62

$3\frac{1}{3}-1\frac{2}{3}=1\frac{2}{3}$

$5\frac{1}{5}-3\frac{4}{5}=1\frac{2}{5}$

$5\frac{3}{6}-2\frac{4}{6}=2\frac{5}{6}$

$7\frac{2}{8}-4\frac{5}{8}=2\frac{5}{8}$

PAGE 63

$3\frac{7}{8}-1\frac{5}{8}=2\frac{2}{8}$ or $2\frac{1}{4}$

$5\frac{6}{9}-2\frac{2}{9}=3\frac{4}{9}$

$8\frac{3}{5}-5\frac{2}{5}=3\frac{1}{5}$

$6\frac{5}{6}-2\frac{3}{6}=4\frac{2}{6}$ or $4\frac{1}{3}$

$7\frac{9}{10}-2\frac{7}{10}=5\frac{2}{10}$ or $5\frac{1}{5}$

$9\frac{8}{12}-2\frac{6}{12}=7\frac{2}{12}$ or $7\frac{1}{6}$

$7\frac{1}{4}-2\frac{2}{4}=4\frac{3}{4}$

$3\frac{1}{6}-1\frac{2}{6}=1\frac{5}{6}$

$4\frac{6}{9}-1\frac{8}{9}=2\frac{7}{9}$

$9\frac{3}{11}-4\frac{5}{11}=4\frac{9}{11}$

PAGE 64

$3\frac{1}{6}+2\frac{2}{6}=5\frac{3}{6}$ or $5\frac{1}{2}$

$5\frac{2}{5}-2\frac{1}{5}=3\frac{1}{5}$

$6\frac{5}{8}-2\frac{3}{8}=4\frac{2}{8}$ or $4\frac{1}{4}$

$2\frac{2}{7}+2\frac{4}{7}=4\frac{6}{7}$

$3+2\frac{1}{2}=5\frac{1}{2}$

$3\frac{4}{10}-2\frac{2}{10}=1\frac{2}{10}$ or $1\frac{1}{5}$

$7\frac{9}{12}-5\frac{2}{12}=2\frac{7}{12}$

$1\frac{2}{5}+2\frac{2}{5}=3\frac{4}{5}$

$3+3\frac{1}{4}=6\frac{1}{4}$

$2\frac{3}{5}+1\frac{2}{5}=4$

$7+3\frac{5}{8}=10\frac{5}{8}$

$4-2\frac{1}{2}=1\frac{1}{2}$

$8\frac{5}{9}-2\frac{7}{9}=5\frac{7}{9}$

PAGE 65

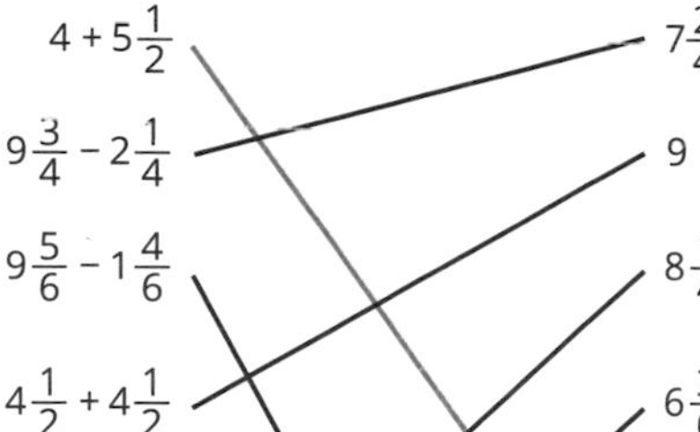

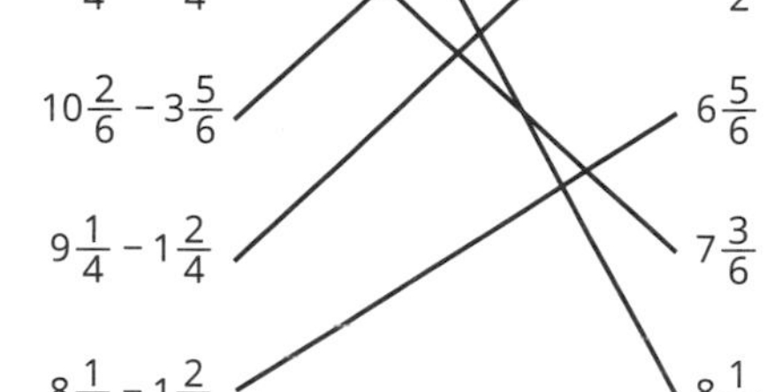

$4 + 5\frac{1}{2}$	$7\frac{2}{4}$
$9\frac{3}{4} - 2\frac{1}{4}$	9
$9\frac{5}{6} - 1\frac{4}{6}$	$8\frac{1}{4}$
$4\frac{1}{2} + 4\frac{1}{2}$	$6\frac{3}{6}$
$3\frac{4}{6} + 3\frac{5}{6}$	$7\frac{3}{4}$
$4\frac{2}{4} + 3\frac{3}{4}$	$9\frac{1}{2}$
$10\frac{2}{6} - 3\frac{5}{6}$	$6\frac{5}{6}$
$9\frac{1}{4} - 1\frac{2}{4}$	$7\frac{3}{6}$
$8\frac{1}{6} - 1\frac{2}{6}$	$8\frac{1}{6}$

PAGE 66

$2\frac{1}{4} + 1\frac{2}{4} = 3\frac{3}{4}$ hours

$2\frac{2}{3} + 3\frac{1}{3} = 6$ tablespoons

$9\frac{3}{8} - 5\frac{7}{8} = 3\frac{4}{8}$ or $3\frac{1}{2}$ gallons

$9\frac{6}{12} - 2\frac{7}{12} = 6\frac{11}{12}$ feet

PAGE 67

$\frac{2}{3} = 2 \times \frac{1}{3}$ | $\frac{3}{4} = 3 \times \frac{1}{4}$

$\frac{3}{5} = 3 \times \frac{1}{5}$ | $\frac{5}{6} = 5 \times \frac{1}{6}$

$\frac{7}{8} = 7 \times \frac{1}{8}$ | $\frac{7}{9} = 7 \times \frac{1}{9}$

PAGE 68

$\frac{3}{10} = 3 \times \frac{1}{10}$ | $\frac{2}{6} = 2 \times \frac{1}{6}$

$\frac{4}{5} = 4 \times \frac{1}{5}$ | $\frac{8}{12} = 8 \times \frac{1}{12}$

$\frac{9}{10} = 9 \times \frac{1}{10}$ | $\frac{5}{9} = 5 \times \frac{1}{9}$

$\frac{5}{8} = 5 \times \frac{1}{8}$ | $\frac{6}{11} = 6 \times \frac{1}{11}$

$\frac{3}{7} = 3 \times \frac{1}{7}$ | $\frac{7}{12} = 7 \times \frac{1}{12}$

PAGE 69

$\frac{3}{8} + \frac{3}{8} = \frac{6}{8}$

$2 \times \frac{3}{8} = \frac{6}{8}$

$\frac{2}{4} + \frac{2}{4} + \frac{2}{4} = \frac{6}{4}$ or $1\frac{1}{2}$

$3 \times \frac{2}{4} = \frac{6}{4}$ or $1\frac{1}{2}$

$\frac{4}{5} + \frac{4}{5} + \frac{4}{5} = \frac{12}{5}$ or $2\frac{2}{5}$

$3 \times \frac{4}{5} = \frac{12}{5}$ or $2\frac{2}{5}$

PAGE 70

$3 \times \frac{5}{8} = \frac{15}{8}$ or $1\frac{7}{8}$

$4 \times \frac{3}{4} = \frac{12}{4}$ or 3

$7 \times \frac{2}{5} = \frac{14}{5}$ or $2\frac{4}{5}$

$6 \times \frac{6}{8} = \frac{36}{8}$ or $4\frac{1}{2}$

PAGE 71

$4 \times \frac{2}{9} = \frac{8}{9}$

$2 \times \frac{3}{5} = \frac{6}{5}$ or $1\frac{1}{5}$

$3 \times \frac{6}{11} = \frac{18}{11}$ or $1\frac{7}{11}$

$5 \times \frac{8}{12} = \frac{40}{12}$ or $3\frac{1}{3}$

$6 \times \frac{9}{10} = \frac{54}{10}$ or $5\frac{2}{5}$

$8 \times \frac{6}{7} = \frac{48}{7}$ or $6\frac{6}{7}$

$7 \times \frac{5}{8} = \frac{35}{8}$ or $4\frac{3}{8}$

$9 \times \frac{11}{12} = \frac{99}{12}$ or $8\frac{1}{4}$

PAGE 72

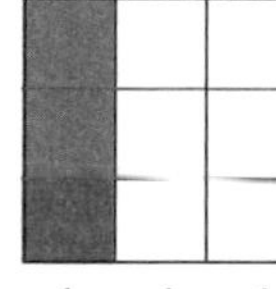

$\frac{1}{3}$ of $\frac{1}{3} = \frac{1}{9}$

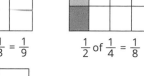

$\frac{1}{2}$ of $\frac{1}{4} = \frac{1}{8}$

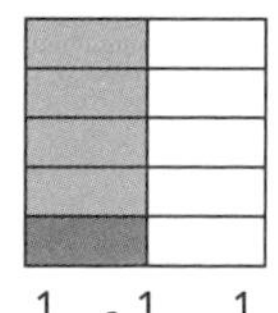

$\frac{1}{5}$ of $\frac{1}{2} = \frac{1}{10}$

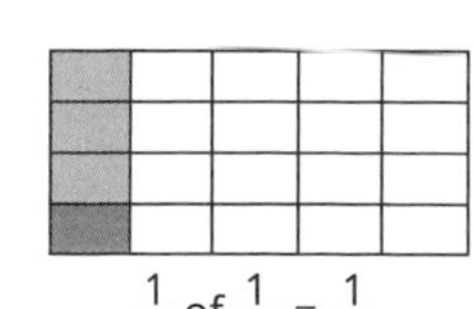

$\frac{1}{4}$ of $\frac{1}{5} = \frac{1}{20}$

PAGE 73

$\frac{1}{5} \times \frac{3}{4} = \frac{3}{20}$ | $\frac{2}{7} \times \frac{3}{5} = \frac{6}{35}$

$\frac{3}{4} \times \frac{1}{4} = \frac{3}{16}$ | $\frac{3}{8} \times \frac{2}{3} = \frac{6}{24}$ or $\frac{1}{4}$

$\frac{4}{5} \times \frac{1}{2} = \frac{4}{10}$ or $\frac{2}{5}$ | $\frac{4}{7} \times \frac{2}{3} = \frac{8}{21}$

PAGE 74

$5 \times \frac{7}{8} = \frac{35}{8}$ or $4\frac{3}{8}$ inches

$4 \times \frac{3}{8} = \frac{12}{8}$ or $1\frac{1}{2}$ tablespoons

$9 \times \frac{5}{8} = \frac{45}{8}$ or $5\frac{5}{8}$ pounds

$7 \times \frac{4}{6} = \frac{28}{6}$ or $4\frac{2}{3}$ hours

Yes. He will practice $7 \times \frac{3}{4} = \frac{21}{4}$ or $5\frac{1}{4}$ hours per week.

PAGE 75

$\frac{5}{8} + \frac{1}{8} = \frac{6}{8}$ or $\frac{3}{4}$

$\frac{10}{12} - \frac{4}{12} = \frac{6}{12}$ or $\frac{1}{2}$

$2 \times \frac{1}{10} = \frac{2}{10}$ or $\frac{1}{5}$

$4 \times \frac{5}{6} = \frac{20}{6}$ or $3\frac{1}{3}$

$\frac{3}{8} + \frac{3}{8} = \frac{6}{8}$ or $\frac{3}{4}$

$\frac{9}{10} - \frac{1}{10} = \frac{8}{10}$ or $\frac{4}{5}$

$2\frac{3}{4} - \frac{1}{4} = 2\frac{2}{4}$ or $2\frac{1}{2}$

$6 \times \frac{4}{3} = \frac{24}{3}$ or 8

$\frac{5}{6} + \frac{3}{6} = \frac{8}{6}$ or $1\frac{1}{3}$

$2\frac{2}{9} - 1\frac{1}{9} = 1\frac{1}{9}$

Answer key

PAGE 76

$\frac{7}{8} - \frac{1}{8}$	$\frac{4}{5} - \frac{2}{5}$
$\frac{2}{12} + \frac{6}{12}$	$3 \times \frac{2}{10}$
$\frac{1}{5} + \frac{1}{5}$	$4 \times \frac{3}{8}$
$\frac{6}{8} + \frac{6}{8}$	$7 \times \frac{1}{10}$
$\frac{2}{10} + \frac{5}{10}$	$\frac{7}{12} + \frac{3}{12}$
$\frac{3}{10} + \frac{3}{10}$	$\frac{4}{12} + \frac{5}{12}$
$\frac{10}{12} - \frac{1}{12}$	$3 \times \frac{2}{8}$
$5 \times \frac{2}{12}$	$\frac{10}{12} - \frac{2}{12}$

PAGE 77

$9 \times \frac{5}{8} = \frac{45}{8}$ or $5\frac{5}{8}$ pounds

$\frac{3}{10} + \frac{6}{10} = \frac{9}{10}$ of the students

$\frac{7}{8} - \frac{4}{8} = \frac{3}{8}$ of a mile

$8 \times \frac{3}{4} = \frac{24}{4}$ or 6 miles

$1 - \frac{5}{12} - \frac{3}{12} = \frac{4}{12}$ or $\frac{1}{3}$ of the class

PAGE 78

$\frac{1}{2}$ mile

$\frac{1}{4}$ of a mile

$\frac{1}{8}$ of mile

Answers will vary. One possible answer is shown below.

The denominator doubles each time. The next few distances will be $\frac{1}{16}$ of a mile, $\frac{1}{32}$ of a mile, and $\frac{1}{64}$ of a mile.

PAGE 79

$\frac{2}{10}$ $\frac{9}{10}$ $\frac{6}{10}$

$\frac{80}{100}$ $\frac{48}{100}$ $\frac{45}{100}$

PAGE 80

$\frac{24}{100} = 0.24$

$\frac{13}{100} = 0.13$

$\frac{9}{10} = 0.9$

$\frac{36}{100} = 0.36$

$\frac{5}{10} = 0.5$

$\frac{4}{10} = 0.4$

$\frac{64}{100} = 0.64$

$\frac{2}{10} = 0.2$

PAGE 81

$1\frac{2}{10} = 1.2$

$\frac{30}{100} = 0.3$ or 0.30

$\frac{65}{100} = 0.65$

$\frac{28}{100} = 0.28$

$\frac{6}{100} = 0.06$

$0.25 = \frac{25}{100}$ or $\frac{1}{4}$

$0.91 = \frac{91}{100}$

$0.85 = \frac{85}{100}$ or $\frac{17}{20}$

$\frac{8}{10} = 0.8$

$\frac{40}{100} = 0.4$ or 0.40

$1\frac{89}{100} = 1.89$

$\frac{4}{100} = 0.04$

$6\frac{5}{100} = 6.05$

$0.7 = \frac{7}{10}$

$0.14 = \frac{14}{100}$ or $\frac{7}{50}$

$0.02 = \frac{2}{100}$ or $\frac{1}{50}$

PAGE 82

$\frac{3}{5} = \frac{6}{10} = 0.6$

$\frac{20}{25} = \frac{80}{100} = 0.8$ or 0.80

$\frac{13}{50} = \frac{26}{100} = 0.26$

$\frac{39}{50} = \frac{78}{100} = 0.78$

$\frac{2}{4} = \frac{50}{100} = 0.5$ or 0.50

$\frac{1}{5} = \frac{20}{100} = 0.2$ or 0.20

PAGE 83

$\frac{2}{50} = 0.04$

$\frac{1}{4} = 0.25$

$\frac{4}{5} = 0.8$

$5\frac{3}{4} = 5.75$

$\frac{8}{25} = 0.32$

$\frac{17}{25} = 0.68$

$\frac{49}{50} = 0.98$

$\frac{20}{50} = 0.4$

$1\frac{5}{25} = 1.2$

$\frac{1}{2} = 0.5$

$\frac{35}{50} = 0.7$

$2\frac{16}{20} = 2.8$

$\frac{13}{20} = 0.65$

$3\frac{37}{50} = 3.74$

PAGE 84

$\frac{3}{5}$	0.12
$\frac{3}{20}$	0.3
$\frac{6}{50}$	0.6
$\frac{4}{5}$	0.48
$\frac{6}{20}$	0.06
$\frac{33}{50}$	0.15
$\frac{2}{5}$	0.4
$\frac{12}{25}$	0.66
$\frac{3}{50}$	0.8

PAGE 85

0.75

0.3

10.5

0.25

2.2

3.5

PAGE 86

A

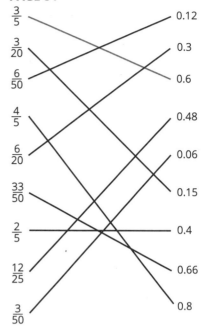

$\frac{5}{10}$	$\frac{10}{25}$	$\frac{4}{10}$	$\frac{2}{20}$	$\frac{3}{50}$
$\frac{30}{50}$	$\frac{20}{25}$	$\frac{1}{25}$	$\frac{17}{20}$	$\frac{2}{10}$
$\frac{2}{5}$	$\frac{43}{100}$	$\frac{8}{20}$	$\frac{19}{25}$	$\frac{13}{20}$
$\frac{4}{5}$	$\frac{2}{25}$	$\frac{15}{25}$	$\frac{19}{20}$	$\frac{7}{50}$
$\frac{4}{50}$	$\frac{6}{20}$	$\frac{49}{100}$	$\frac{61}{100}$	$\frac{7}{10}$
$\frac{3}{5}$	$\frac{59}{100}$	$\frac{9}{20}$	$\frac{4}{20}$	$\frac{31}{50}$

B

PAGE 87

0.16 < 0.5   0.52 > 0.25

0.7 < 0.9   0.8 > 0.08

0.3 = 0.30   0.5 < 0.53

PAGE 88

0.6 < 0.68   0.87 > 0.78

0.51 < 0.59   0.09 < 0.1

0.12 < 0.2   0.20 = 0.2

0.24   0.4   2.4

0.18   1.8   8.1

0.1   0.18   0.81

0.07   0.7   0.77

PAGE 89

Piping Pepper Hot Sauce

The blue paper clip

The silver phone

Too big

PAGE 90

$0.15 + 0.37 = 0.52$ $0.79 + 0.01 = 0.80$

$0.23 + 0.34 = 0.57$ $0.34 + 0.63 = 0.97$

$1.56 + 0.54 = 2.10$ $1.53 + 0.77 = 2.30$

$1.97 + 4.82 = 6.79$ $8.83 + 9.59 = 18.42$

PAGE 91

$0.50 + 0.24 = 0.74$ $0.30 + 0.48 = 0.78$

$4.60 + 0.21 = 4.81$ $2.35 + 0.70 = 3.05$

$1.72 + 0.30 = 2.02$ $1.38 + 0.90 = 2.28$

$0.99 + 0.10 = 1.09$ $0.70 + 4.57 = 5.27$

PAGE 92

$0.45 - 0.12 = 0.33$ $0.28 - 0.04 = 0.24$

$0.29 - 0.25 = 0.04$ $0.64 - 0.51 = 0.13$

$2.68 - 0.35 = 2.33$ $1.68 - 0.49 = 1.19$

$2.34 - 1.89 = 0.45$ $5.63 - 2.35 = 3.28$

PAGE 93

$0.78 - 0.40 = 0.38$ $0.31 - 0.20 = 0.11$

$1.65 - 0.40 = 1.25$ $3.59 - 0.70 = 2.89$

$2.60 - 0.31 = 2.29$ $4.18 - 0.60 = 3.58$

$3.57 - 1.70 = 1.87$ $1.97 - 1.89 = 0.08$

PAGE 94

$6.75 + $2.85 = $9.60

$5.50 + $1.99 = $7.49

$9.60 + $7.49 = $17.09

$17.09 − $0.90 = $16.19

$20.00 − $16.19 = $3.81

PAGE 95

0.45 + 0.21 = 0.66   0.95 − 0.6 = 0.35

1.98 − 0.09 = 1.89   1.96 − 0.8 = 1.16

1.7 + 0.44 = 2.14   1.23 + 0.9 = 2.13

4.88 − 2.98 = 1.9   1.7 − 0.84 = 0.86

PAGE 96

$\frac{2}{5} + \frac{1}{5} = \frac{3}{5}$

$2 + \frac{3}{4} = \frac{11}{4}$ or $2\frac{3}{4}$

$\frac{5}{12} + \frac{6}{12} = \frac{11}{12}$

$1\frac{2}{7} + \frac{4}{7} = 1\frac{6}{7}$

$2\frac{1}{6} + \frac{3}{6} = 2\frac{4}{6}$ or $2\frac{2}{3}$

$\frac{4}{9} + \frac{5}{9} = \frac{9}{9}$ or 1

$2\frac{4}{10} + \frac{8}{10} = 3\frac{2}{10}$ or $3\frac{1}{5}$

$1\frac{4}{5} + 2\frac{3}{5} = 4\frac{2}{5}$

$\frac{6}{8} - \frac{3}{8} = \frac{3}{8}$

$\frac{4}{5} - \frac{1}{5} = \frac{3}{5}$

$\frac{10}{11} - \frac{3}{11} = \frac{7}{11}$

$\frac{11}{12} - \frac{9}{12} = \frac{2}{12}$ or $\frac{1}{6}$

$3\frac{5}{7} - \frac{3}{7} = 3\frac{2}{7}$

$5\frac{3}{4} - 1\frac{1}{4} = 4\frac{2}{4}$ or $4\frac{1}{2}$

$3\frac{1}{3} - 1\frac{1}{3} = 2$

PAGE 97

$\frac{2}{5} + \frac{2}{5} = \frac{4}{5}$ $\frac{7}{8} - \frac{2}{8} = \frac{5}{8}$

$\frac{1}{7} + \frac{3}{7} = \frac{4}{7}$ $\frac{5}{9} + \frac{7}{9} = \frac{12}{9}$

$2\frac{1}{8} - \frac{3}{8} = 1\frac{6}{8}$ $1\frac{5}{9} + \frac{2}{9} = 1\frac{7}{9}$

$3\frac{7}{12} - 1\frac{6}{12} = 2\frac{1}{12}$ $1\frac{2}{4} + 1\frac{3}{4} = 3\frac{1}{4}$

$\frac{4}{5} - \frac{1}{5} = \frac{3}{5}$ $\frac{5}{8} - \frac{2}{8} = \frac{3}{8}$

$1\frac{4}{5} + \frac{1}{5} = 2$ $1\frac{4}{9} - 1\frac{2}{9} = \frac{2}{9}$

$1\frac{5}{8} + 1\frac{2}{8} = 2\frac{7}{8}$ $\frac{5}{10} + 1\frac{4}{10} = 1\frac{9}{10}$

$6\frac{8}{9} - 2\frac{5}{9} = 4\frac{3}{9}$ $1\frac{1}{10} + \frac{2}{10} = 1\frac{3}{10}$

Answer key

PAGE 98

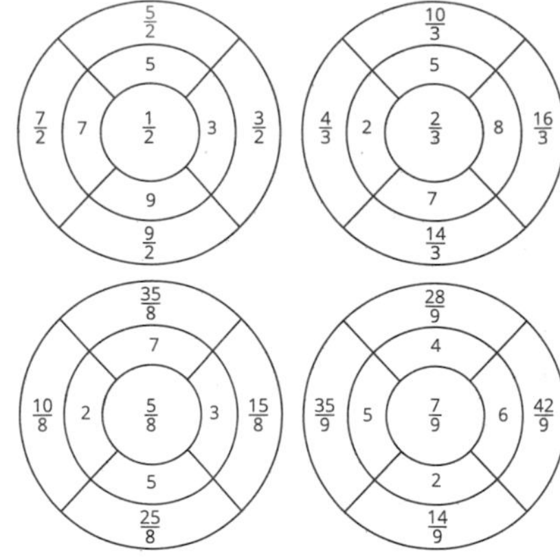

PAGE 99

$\frac{37}{100} = 0.37$

$\frac{3}{10} = 0.3$

$\frac{7}{100} = 0.07$

$\frac{4}{5} = 0.8$

$\frac{1}{4} = 0.25$

$\frac{16}{50} = 0.32$

$\frac{19}{25} = 0.76$

$\frac{29}{50} = 0.58$

$\frac{17}{20} = 0.85$

$0.49 = \frac{49}{100}$

$0.5 = \frac{5}{10}$ or $\frac{1}{2}$

$0.56 = \frac{56}{100}$ or $\frac{14}{25}$

$0.09 = \frac{9}{100}$

$0.2 = \frac{2}{10}$ or $\frac{1}{5}$

$0.28 = \frac{28}{100}$ or $\frac{7}{25}$

$0.18 = \frac{18}{100}$ or $\frac{9}{50}$

$0.05 = \frac{5}{100}$ or $\frac{1}{20}$

$0.88 = \frac{88}{100}$ or $\frac{22}{25}$

PAGE 100

$\frac{9}{10} - \frac{3}{10} = \frac{6}{10}$ or $\frac{3}{5}$

$\frac{4}{8} + \frac{2}{8} = \frac{6}{8}$ or $\frac{3}{4}$

$5 \times \frac{6}{7} = \frac{30}{7}$ or $4\frac{2}{7}$

0.9 − 0.4 = 0.5

0.25 + 0.11 = 0.36

$\frac{29}{5} - \frac{17}{5} = \frac{12}{5}$ or $2\frac{2}{5}$

$1\frac{2}{3} + \frac{2}{3} = 2\frac{1}{3}$

0.65 − 0.2 = 0.45

$2\frac{5}{12} - 1\frac{3}{12} = 1\frac{2}{12}$ or $1\frac{1}{6}$

$3\frac{3}{5} + 2\frac{3}{5} = 6\frac{1}{5}$

1.18 − 0.48 = 0.70 or 0.7

0.34 + 0.89 = 1.23

PAGE 101

$8 \times \frac{6}{9} = \frac{48}{9}$ or $5\frac{1}{3}$

0.38 − 0.29 = 0.09

0.77 + 0.14 = 0.91

$6\frac{1}{4} - 1\frac{1}{4} = 5$

$6\frac{1}{5} + 2\frac{2}{5} = 8\frac{3}{5}$

$12 \times \frac{2}{9} = \frac{24}{9}$ or $2\frac{2}{3}$

1.5 + 0.31 = 1.81

$2\frac{1}{7} - 1\frac{4}{7} = \frac{4}{7}$

2.25 − 0.71 = 1.54

$6 \times \frac{5}{6} = \frac{30}{6}$ or 5

0.8 − 0.19 = 0.61

0.67 + 0.4 = 1.07

0.42 + 1.09 = 1.51

$4\frac{1}{9} - 2\frac{2}{9} = 1\frac{8}{9}$

PAGE 102

49.4 pounds

$\frac{1}{4}$ of a foot

$7.26

21 students

PAGE 103

5.03 pounds of fruit

9 jars

$4.75

$\frac{21}{16}$ or $1\frac{5}{16}$ gallons